Leadership in High-Performance Organizational Cultures

Leadership in High-Performance Organizational Cultures

STANLEY D. TRUSKIE

QUORUM BOOKS
Westport, Connecticut • London

HD57.7
.T78
1999

Library of Congress Cataloging-in-Publication Data

Truskie, Stanley D.
    Leadership in high-performance organizational cultures / Stanley
D. Truskie.
        p.   cm.
    Includes bibliographical references and index.
    ISBN 1–56720–236–5 (alk. paper)
    1. Leadership.   2. Corporate culture.   I. Title.
HD57.7.T78   1999
    658.4'092—dc21   98–51664

British Library Cataloguing in Publication Data is available.

Library of Congress Catalog Card Number: 98–51664
ISBN: 1–56720–236–5

First published in 1999

Quorum Books, 88 Post Road West, Westport, CT 06881
An imprint of Greenwood Publishing Group, Inc.
www.quorumbooks.com

Printed in the United States of America

The paper used in this book complies with the
Permanent Paper Standard issued by the National
Information Standards Organization (Z39.48–1984).

10 9 8 7 6 5 4 3 2

This book is dedicated to my family members,
who have provided me with the
love, support, and inspiration
that have helped me complete this project:
Marianne
Mark
Lynn
Craig
Brian

Contents

Figures

Preface

As a leadership/organization development professional, I have been studying leadership and organizations for a long time. Similar to the search for the Holy Grail, I have been searching for the treasure that would uncover the "truth" about effective leadership—the knowledge that would shed light on the key leadership factors that help a person run an organization successfully. I knew if I could find that treasure, it would help make my job of leadership development more effective and more rewarding.

After spending 25-plus years of practicing leadership development, conducting applied research, and studying others' findings, I have concluded this: all the evidence overwhelmingly suggests that there is a direct link between *leadership*, *organizational culture*, and *performance*. To elaborate, the findings support the concept that a leader can have an impact on forming the culture of an organization, which further can have an enhancing effect of improving the level, ensuring the consistency, and sustaining the duration of the organization's continuous performance improvement. In short, a leader can improve the immediate and long-term performance of his/her organization by forming the right culture. So the key for leaders (or leaders-to-be) is to know and understand organizational culture, to know what a performance-enhancing culture is, and to have some idea about the role leadership plays in forming a performance-enhancing culture.

But I find that, instead of focusing on this aspect of leadership, leaders are focusing on another area—leadership style. They tend to struggle with the issue of searching for an optimal leadership style—one that is compatible with who they are (personality and character) and, at the same time, one that meets the requirements of effective leadership. In searching for their optimal style, many have the misconception that there is an "ideal" personality that lends itself to great leadership. Many believe, for example, that all great leaders possess the quality of charisma—a special magnetic charm or appeal. They are often surprised when I point out that while it is true that charisma can have a positive effect on leadership, it is also true that the most charismatic leader can be a disaster to the organization he/she leads.

So if it is true that leadership, organizational culture, and performance are closely linked, what do we know about leaders in general relative to this connection? The important lessons I have learned in studying and working with exceptional chief executives and other top executives are these:

1. There is no *one* particular leadership style that distinguishes effective from less effective leaders. For example, among participative leaders I have found some to be very effective in leading their organizations, while others have been very ineffective.

2. Every leader, even the most effective ones, has some flaw, weakness, or deficiency. There is no such thing as a perfect leader; there are only very good ones.

3. What seems to distinguish effective leaders from their less effective counterparts is their level of awareness of and willingness to acknowledge their weaknesses. Effective leaders use this awareness to ensure that their weaknesses do not transcend the organization and affect it in a negative way.

Further, exceptional leaders feel a strong sense of duty to look beyond personal, self-centered interests to create an effective organization, one in which members feel needed and are able to contribute to the success of the organization. To accomplish this, exceptional leaders have an organizational leadership strategy—a guiding plan that creates an internal environment; a culture that is healthy, balanced, and adaptive. These leaders strive to form a culture that enables members to achieve superior, long-term performance.

The strategy of these exceptional leaders is what this book is all about. It is written to be of help to anyone who has the challenging responsibility of leading others and who has a desire to create an organization (company, division, department) that is a "standout" performer which achieves extraordinary results on a consistent basis. It is based on my extensive experience and the findings I have uncovered as I have developed and refined my approach to helping individuals become effective leaders.

I have used this strategy in helping leaders, at all levels, improve the performance of their organizations and achieve exceptional results. I have studied successful organizations which have followed the principles of this strategy and achieved similar positive results. In summary, the organizational leadership strategy presented in this book can greatly enhance the leadership performance of those who learn it and put it to use.

WHO SHOULD READ THIS BOOK?

This book is written for several audiences. The first and most important are leaders (i.e., presidents, vice presidents, directors, administrators, managers, and supervisors). Anyone who has been given the responsibility of leading others has two important tasks to carry out: (1) to provide direction to others (i.e., to determine where the organization is going, to explain why it's going in that direction, and to communicate how it's going to get there); and (2) to develop an effective organization that will enable members of the organization to move in that direction.

Every leader in an organization has essentially the same two tasks to carry out, albeit at various levels of complexity and difficulty. The ideas, methods, and techniques described in this book can be applied to a unit, department, division, or the entire company. Ideally, it would be most effective if applied throughout the company; however, I am a realist, and I understand that the politics and bureaucracy of an organization oftentimes stand in the way of organization-wide change. However, this should not stop a leader from moving ahead to improve the performance of his/ her unit, department, or division.

The book should also benefit those who help and support leaders. Human resource professionals, leadership trainers, organizational development specialists, consultants, executive/management development specialists, business school faculty, and organizational psychologists are among those who will find this book useful as a resource to supplement material they are currently using.

Students who have an interest in leadership and who are attempting to gain a perspective that incorporates organizational culture should also benefit from this book. The contents represent many different disciplines in supporting the concepts and approaches presented. For example, the book draws from the fields of business, management, general psychology, organizational psychology, sociology, and anthropology, just to name a few. The overall purpose is more toward the application of principles representing several disciplines as they relate to leadership and organizational culture, rather than an in-depth scholarly study of each. References are presented that should be helpful to those seeking a more in-depth study of each area.

OVERVIEW OF THE CONTENTS

The book is presented in twelve chapters. Chapter 1 begins with an explanation of how I was motivated to develop a leadership model that would be helpful to leaders as the health, fitness, and nutrition model I discovered was helpful to me. The chapter goes on to describe the leadership model which I term the L^4 strategy.

Chapter 2 describes the L^4 strategy as a leadership guide to be used in forming an integrated, balanced culture that can lead to superior performance, consistent results, and sustained growth of the organization. The chapter includes information on the positive, core elements of four cultural patterns and the institutions from which these patterns are drawn.

How the elements are brought together and integrated into the organization to form balance is explained in Chapter 3. Successful, high-performance companies who follow the principles of the L^4 strategy are presented.

Chapter 4 presents information on companies whose cultures are unbalanced. It describes the four directions of unbalanced cultures and gives examples of how these companies experience sub-par performance, underachievement, and slow or no growth.

Chapter 5 focuses on what it takes to become an L^4 leader. It explains the difference between leadership presence and leadership style and how presence is influenced through the combination of one's thinking system and one's personal leadership paradigm. The chapter explains how one can adapt the L^4 strategy into one's leadership repertoire.

Chapter 6 shifts to the concept of establishing direction for the organization. Here the essence of leadership is defined as two tasks: (1) establishing organizational direction, and (2) developing organizational effectiveness. The interdependency of these two tasks is discussed and is supported by examples of those companies who did, and those who did not effectively perform both tasks.

Chapter 7 focuses on the importance of how people and organizations change. It presents findings from the field of psychology that help explain why organizational change initiatives succeed or fail. It is provided as background information to help in preparing an organization to implement the L^4 strategy.

Chapter 8 focuses on the "how-to's" of implementing the L^4 strategy. It stresses the importance that value statements and reinforcing mechanisms play in implementing the L^4 strategy.

Chapter 9 describes the Double G Coatings Company, L.P., and how it implemented and maintains the L^4 strategy. The purpose of this chapter is to give an example of how a young company can institute the L^4 strategy at its early stages of start-up.

Chapter 10 focuses on the concept of organizational conflict and uses the L^4 strategy to explain the cause (and cure) of organizational conflict. It describes why conflict problems arise with organizations (e.g., department to department) and between organizations (e.g., mergers and acquisitions).

Chapter 11 describes the personal attributes that should be used in the selection and development of leaders. This chapter explains how personal attributes required for effective leadership can be developed through training, education, and experience.

Chapter 12 presents a summary of the major points of the book.

ACKNOWLEDGMENTS

I owe considerable thanks to a large number of leaders and professionals with whom I have worked and learned much. I just hope I have given as much in return. I wish I could pay tribute to each one by name, but it is not feasible to do so. I would, however, like to mention several individuals who have made an impact on my life. I consider these individuals to be my friends as well as colleagues who have helped me personally and professionally. These individuals include Sam Moore, John Turyan, H. B. Kincaid, Bob Mill, Herb Gordon, John Guydan, Greg Spencer, and Fr. John Ayoob.

I am grateful to my family for their love and support and to my two brothers, Leon and Ron, for their longtime, big brothers' love and encouragement.

I am also grateful to Dr. Jennifer Ashley for her review and comments on my early manuscript; and I am deeply indebted to my assistant, Lynn Brown, who has provided outstanding dedication and professionalism in performing a wide range of tasks that helped me to do my work, conduct my research, and write articles as well as this book.

Leadership in High-Performance Organizational Cultures

1

In Search of a Model
for Developing Leaders

I am fascinated with how people change. I guess that's not surprising coming from someone who has spent much of his career helping thousands of executives, managers, and supervisors change to become more effective at what they do—leading others. Whether I am conducting a leadership workshop, working one-on-one with a problem manager, or counseling an executive on personal leadership improvement, the level of success I achieve is measured in terms of the extent to which I am able to help these individuals develop their leadership potential and achieve greater personal fulfillment, competence, and satisfaction.

In helping people change and improve, I have turned to many different behavioral change methods and techniques. Some have worked well while others have not. However, I have found one particular change strategy to be especially effective. I don't have a fancy name for it, and I won't proclaim that it is a breakthrough in learning psychology. It was more or less hidden in my closet of common sense, and I discovered it through a transformation I personally experienced.

It all began about 15 years ago, when I started to become seriously concerned about my personal health and fitness. Like many others approaching the age of 40, I found myself somewhat overweight and out of shape. Although I wasn't technically obese, I did notice I was gaining a few pounds each year. A simple calculation yielded a forecast that predicted I would be 25 to 30 pounds overweight within ten years unless I did something about it. After many attempts at different dieting/fitness programs, I finally discovered one that met my needs. It was a book based on sound, fundamental principles of nutrition and the health sciences. It was interesting to read and easy to understand. It provided me a practical and easy-to-follow guide to help me select the right amounts and combinations of regular foods that were nutritionally sound and healthy. It also included some practical guidelines on physical fitness. This program has helped me control my weight, maintain a high energy level, and improve my general health.

This personal experience unlocked my closet of common sense—it suddenly occurred to me that executives and managers face the same types of struggles in searching for a leadership strategy as I did in searching for a health/fitness strategy. Like me, they are constantly bombarded with books, tapes, and programs promoting various management theories, techniques, processes, and approaches. Like me, they become so overloaded with information that they become confused and, therefore, unable to develop a coherent, unified strategy to follow in guiding their leadership performance. This insight led me to the realization that executives and managers needed a practical and useful model that would help guide their leadership strategy the same way the health/fitness model guided mine. I also realized that if this strategy was to work for them as mine worked for me, it would have to have the same qualities and characteristics as mine did (i.e., it had to be research-based, not overly complicated, practical; and it had to demonstrate positive results).

I have developed a leadership model that meets these criteria. I refer to it as the L^4 strategy. It is logical and simple to understand, yet profound in how it can enhance one's leadership performance. It explains why some organizations succeed while others underperform and fail. It clearly demonstrates the importance of leadership, at all levels, in determining the fate of the organization. It provides an explanation of how one's leadership style differs from leadership presence and why a style may be difficult, if not impossible, to change. The L^4 strategy offers alternatives in attempting to change leaders' personalities to improve leadership performance, and it offers practical guidance for improving organizational performance. Finally, it offers a powerful strategy that will help leaders strengthen their organization in the midst of a rapidly changing social and economic environment.

I have used the L^4 strategy to help executives and managers improve their organizations' performances. Its power has also been demonstrated by successful, fast-growth companies as well as established companies who have transformed themselves from underperformers to high achievers.

The L^4 strategy is an organizational leadership strategy that is intended to form an integrated and balanced culture. The L^4 strategy draws upon positive elements from four institutional groupings and integrates them into the existing culture. These institutional groupings include (1) the family, (2) social institutions, (3) the scientific community, and (4) the military/law enforcement establishments. As positive elements from each of these groupings are integrated into the existing culture, the culture becomes balanced and adaptive. In other words, the formed culture exhibits positive characteristics of each of these institutional groupings that enables it to gain organizational benefits of each. For example, when the positive elements of family (caring, sharing, and teamwork), social institutions (human growth and development), the scientific community (achievement and advancement), and the military/law establishments (consistency and efficiency) are integrated in a balanced way, the resulting culture's performance is enhanced.

The L^4 strategy is an organizational leadership strategy; it should not be confused with a directional leadership strategy. Directional leadership strategy deals with the direction of the organization. It usually consists of a vision or the future aspirations of the firm, its mission or purpose, performance objectives, and a business plan designed to meet established goals and objectives. Essentially, a directional leadership strategy establishes the directional intent of the organization, while the organizational leadership strategy enables it to move in the intended direction. It has been my experience that while most leaders have a defined directional leadership strategy in place, many lack an accompanying coherent and defined organizational leadership strategy. The L^4 strategy provides the missing link to fill this leadership void. It is based on the preponderance of evidence that supports the notion that integrating positive elements of the four institutional groupings previously mentioned into an existing culture enhances its performance capabilities.

In order to understand an integrated and balanced culture and how it contributes to successful and consistent performance more fully, it is instructive to review what we know about leadership, organizational culture, and performance. In other words, is there scientific evidence to support a cause-and-effect relationship between and among these three important factors?

The answer to that question requires a review of recent findings on organizational leadership. With one exception, not much that can be considered new or significant regarding organizational leadership has been uncovered during the past 30 years. That exception is what could be considered to be one of the most important breakthroughs in understanding the impact of leadership on organizational performance. It started during the 1980s when management scholars and academics began to study culture in organizations and its impact on organizational performance.[1] The results of these efforts led to the discovery of the extent to which organizational culture can and does affect organizational performance and the impact that leadership has on forming the culture of the organization.[2]

Although this critically important information on leadership has been available for some time, it has been obscured due to the method and format of its dissemination. It has mostly been shared between and among academics, scholars, and high brow consulting firms. Practical leaders outside these circles did not fully understand and appreciate the significance of these findings because they have been presented in theoretical and abstract models accompanied by language that was equally abstract and ponderous—all of which is a turnoff to leaders of the business world. When attempts have been made to bring it down to a practical level, it has been presented in soft and fuzzy language that is alien and even offensive to practicing managers.[3] So unfortunately, the most potentially important and useful information on organizational leadership has been and continues to go largely ignored among the community of practicing leaders (executives, managers, and supervisors). If it is to be found anywhere in the organization, it will probably be found in a 300-page textbook sitting on the coffee table in the executive suite.[4]

The L^4 strategy recognizes and applies the principles and important findings on organizational culture and performance within the framework of a practical leadership model. It focuses on the core findings which are helpful, useful, and practical to leaders—at all levels of the organization; and it is presented in a language that is void of obtuse technical language found in highly theoretical treatments of the subject.

I have attempted to apply my extensive years of experience as a leadership consultant in sifting through and boiling down all the pertinent research and writings to some major principles which I have found to be practical and usable in the real world of business and work. If the reader is interested in a more in-depth look at leadership and organizational culture, I have provided extensive notes in the back of the book with suggested readings. Much of what is presented throughout the book is supported by references listed there.

2

The L⁴ Strategy: Forming a Performance-Enhancing Culture

The study of organizational culture is rooted in the broad study of cultures throughout civilization and originates from social anthropology. Studies conducted in the late nineteenth and early twentieth centuries focused on "primitive" societies—Eskimo, South Sea, African, Native American—and revealed ways of life that were not only different from the more technically advanced parts of America and Europe but among themselves as well.[1]

The study of culture focuses on the shared values and beliefs of a society's members in order to gain an understanding of their actions and behaviors. It is these collective shared beliefs and values that shape group-behavior norms (a pervasive way of acting that is found in a group) which ultimately define a given culture.[2]

Group-behavior norms are not imposed on others by formalized, written rules but are learned by new members as they begin to understand what is acceptable and what is not acceptable behavior. Acceptable behavior is rewarded while unacceptable behavior is sanctioned. Those who conform fit in while those who don't are treated as outsiders.[3]

Organizational culture in its simplest definition is "the set of members' beliefs about the way we do business around here." It is the values and practices shared across all groups in an organization. In a practical sense, it involves the employees, their assumptions about work, the customer, and each other. It is a powerful force in shaping employee behavior, and it has proven to be a significant factor in promoting or inhibiting organizational performance.[4]

Those who have studied organizational culture have revealed some important findings. Among those of significance are the following:

Figure 2.1
The L⁴ Strategy

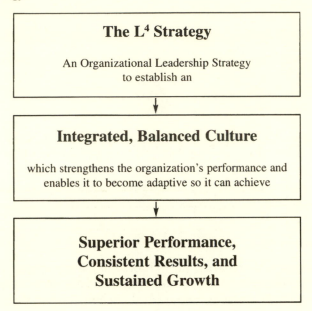

* Organizational culture has been shown to have a direct link to organizational performance.[5]
* Organizational culture and leadership are closely connected. The shaping and management of culture are the essence of leadership.[6]
* Leaders tend to shape their organizational cultures according to their personal preferences and guiding beliefs. They develop a picture of how things ought to be and build the organization according to their basic assumptions about how to run an organization.[7]

The conclusion of these findings plus other related findings strongly suggest that successful organizations have well-defined, integrated, and balanced cultures. Leaders must, therefore, overcome their personal preferences and develop an organizational leadership strategy to establish a balanced and integrated culture.[8] This in essence is the L⁴ strategy, which is illustrated in Figure 2.1.

Ultimately, the goal of the L⁴ strategy is to form a well-defined, integrated, and balanced culture that exerts positive influence on the behaviors of its employees. In such an organization, the employees know and believe in the vision of the company and are emotionally committed to the core values that enhance the attainment of its mission.[9]

THE INTEGRATED AND BALANCED CULTURE

Organizational cultures take time to evolve. Patterns of consistent behavior (group behavior norms) do not emerge overnight. A newer organization, in its early stage of development, may not have as strong and embedded a culture as an organization that has been around for some time. But, even an organization that has been around for years may not have a strong culture. In other words, an older, more mature organization may not have a well-developed culture, meaning there are no noticeable group-behavior norms that run throughout the organization or that different group-behavior norms exist in different parts of the organization (subcultures). Having no organizational culture or a weak one means the absence of an integrated, balanced culture; a strong culture can be either integrated and balanced, or unbalanced. The goal for leaders should be to form a strong, balanced culture by integrating appropriate "characteristics" which are described in the following sections.[10]

The group-behavior norms of an organization are separated into characteristics or "elements" that describe the type of culture that exists.[11] For example, unwritten rules like "never disagree with the boss," "be a team player," "never deviate from standard procedures," or "always tell the truth, no matter how bad" are elements that are used to describe how a culture functions. The origin of these elements can be traced back through the history of the organization, and these elements are perpetuated through various means, with the leader playing a major role in validating or changing the elements.[12]

These elements may be viewed as having either a positive or negative effect on the performance of an organization. For example, the element "being a team player" can have a positive effect in that members share, cooperate, and work together toward the betterment of the organization. On the other hand, the element "never disagree with the boss" can have a negative effect, especially in cases where employees have more information and superior approaches to how jobs or projects should be completed.

An integrated and balanced culture requires that "positive elements" are at work in the organization. The culture is said to be integrated when these positive elements complement rather than oppose one another. The culture is balanced in the sense that positive elements are in place and operating, and no one set of elements is dominating over other important positive elements.[13]

What are the sources of these positive elements? Where can they be found? How are they defined for a particular organization? Positive elements are found in four basic institutional groupings which essentially shape our sociocultural norms. These groupings include (1) the family, (2) social institutions, (3) the scientific community, and (4) the military/law enforcement establishments.[14] Organizations within these institutional groupings have had much to do with the values and beliefs that each of us has adopted, which influences our individual attitudes and behaviors. It is these institutions that represent the four cultural patterns and contain the positive elements for shaping an integrated and balanced culture.

The L[4] strategy is essentially an organizational leadership strategy (L) that uses the positive elements of the previously mentioned institutional cultures in forming an integrated and balanced culture. By integrating these elements in a balanced way, the performance potential of an organization is enhanced—by the power of four. The following is a description of the cultures of these four institutional groupings that offer the positive elements for forming a performance-enhancing culture. By positive elements I mean those that represent the positive values which are at the heart or core of the culture representing each institutional grouping.[15] While other management writers have used similar cultural models and descriptions, the names I have selected are intended to represent only the positive elements at the core of the culture of each institutional grouping.[16]

THE COOPERATION CULTURE

This cultural pattern stems from the term "collectivism," which is rooted in family values, especially those of Asia, South America, and Southern Europe. Family settings of these cultures stress subordinating personal goals to the goals of the group (as opposed to "individualism").[17] Self is defined as part of the group and values harmony and long-term relationships. Member socialization develops a greater commitment to cooperative efforts and creates a positive concern for collective interests. Members who belong describe feelings such as "sense of belonging," "closeness," "accepted," "I felt I was important," "people took me seriously," "respected," and "we took credit for our work as a team."

Like family, the foundation of the *cooperation* culture is trust, caring for one another, helping one another, and sharing. It involves giving up personal interests and doing what is in the best interest of the organization. No one individual stands above what is in the best interest of the group or organization.

Teamwork is the hallmark of the cooperation culture. Individuals and groups strive to help each other. Relationships are very important, as is open communication. Members approach and solve problems together. Interpersonal conflicts are dealt with openly and constructively.

The cooperation culture's emphasis is on consensus, cohesion, and team building. Development of commitment between members and between the members and the organization is stressed. There is a great emphasis on information sharing and participative decision making. This reflects the team concept that the whole is greater than the sum of its parts, meaning you get more when people cooperate. People are not seen as isolated individuals but as cooperating members of a common social system. It has been shown time and again that work teams will consistently outperform work groups.[18]

The cooperation culture seeks diversity because the strength of teams is represented by their diversity. People with varying backgrounds and capabilities offer differing viewpoints and approaches to problems. Teams take the time and effort to recognize individual differences and use them constructively. These differences are not seen as nuisances but as varying perspectives that add value to the team.

An important characteristic of the cooperation culture is its commitment to the whole organization. In return, cooperation culture organizations have a deep commitment to their members and will do all they can to hold on to them. This mutual commitment makes for a strong and lasting bond that involves loyalty both ways.

People are held together by a sense of affiliation and belonging. People work hard at sharing ideas, information, and competencies. When sharing occurs, members find their influence increases. The more opportunities they acquire to be influential, the more competencies they will develop to be more influential. Individualism and self-interests are discouraged in a cooperation culture. Individuals who want to become important or get ahead at the expense of others are not tolerated.

Cooperation and sharing exceed the boundaries of this culture. It seeks to develop cooperative partnerships with stakeholders, including customers and vendors. It invites stakeholders to participate in the development of mission, business plans, and policies. It stresses win/win situations with those who do business with the organization.

People interaction is key in a cooperation culture. Members talk a lot, interact a lot, and meet a lot. They talk to each other and to other team members. Members spend time with each other, on and off the job. Cooperation cultures truly believe in their human resources. They tap the many talents of members by offering opportunities for people to become involved, thereby increasing their influence. Members are encouraged to speak up and say what is on their minds rather than figuring out the "right" thing to say. Members feel safe and free to be open with one another.

"Who you know" in a cooperation culture is not as important as the ideas and concepts you bring to the team. Status and rank take a back seat in the cooperation culture. If you need information or assistance, you are free to contact the individual who can help, regardless of his/her status or rank in the organization.

"Trust is the toughest thing to gain and the easiest to lose"—that is the philosophy of the cooperation culture. Great efforts are made to eliminate politics, infighting, and backstabbing. The cooperation culture strives for honesty by creating an open, informal environment. Leaders work hard to gain members' trust by eliminating barriers to open and honest communications. Straight, honest talk characterizes the way leaders act, and they model this behavior throughout the organization. Self-serving actions and self-important behaviors are seldom seen in leaders of a cooperation culture. The leaders are usually seen as mentors or facilitators.[19]

THE INSPIRATION CULTURE

The *inspiration* cultural pattern emanates from social institutions (religious organizations, social agencies, and charitable institutions). Members of this culture are inspired to achieve because they fervently believe in and are dedicated to this culture's values of humanism, social responsibility, and individual potential.[20]

The inspiration culture is driven by "doing good," or improving the human condition by making things better than they were before. This culture attempts to make a contribution to society. It attempts to build moral content into its purpose or mission. It strives to be a model citizen.[21] It is a culture of mercy or compassion. This translates into developing people, recognizing what people contribute, responding to family and community problems, and sourcing from disadvantaged groups.

The inspiration culture understands and appreciates the aspirations of its members. This culture believes that humans have a great need to grow beyond their current state and reach higher levels of achievement. The focus is on intrinsic rewards which include growth, achievement, affiliation, and self-actualization.[22]

The inspiration culture is known as a dynamic and exciting place that has a high degree of flexibility and individuality. Self-leadership is fostered in that it involves a belief in one's work that extends beyond the formal reward system and relates to the importance of shared organizational vision.[23]

The inspiration culture is usually highly participative and consists of open communication, empowerment of members, and establishment of trust. It emphasizes self-control and self-management, believing that involvement-oriented approaches provide members with challenges and responsibilities that help them grow and develop.

This culture views each person as a unique individual capable of self-mastery and control. It realizes its responsibility to develop the potential competencies of its members. It believes that organizations exist for the individual and not vice versa. It values self-governance, self-control, individual uniqueness, and the right of individuals to make decisions that affect them personally.

The inspiration culture strives to improve the quality of life for its employees and society in general. The future is seen with great hopes for bigger and better things to come. Members are encouraged to reach higher and expand their own and others' horizons. Inspiration cultures usually advance a cause, give to charity, or volunteer time in helping others because they believe in making a contribution to humanity.

Individual growth and development are an important part of the inspiration culture. Since the key value is to nurture potential and broaden people's horizons, individual members are encouraged and supported to seek personal improvement and development. Learning is an individual as well as a shared experience. This culture fosters the free flow of ideas and initiatives among its members.

The inspiration culture believes that empowering members increases individual motivation and, eventually, organizational performance. People are given considerable personal freedom and autonomy. Individuals are given opportunities to explore, discover, and experiment. Risk taking is tolerated because telling people they cannot make mistakes runs counter to what this culture is all about. Negative criticism is banned from this culture because it has a diminishing effect on people and because this culture values expansion of individual and group potential.

THE ACHIEVEMENT CULTURE

The *achievement* cultural pattern is based on the values of the scientific community (this includes all scientific, technical, and research organizations). These institutions play a significant role in the discovery and advancement of new knowledge, new theories, and new technologies. They constantly strive to be at the "leading edge."

Achievement, through research and discovery, embodies the essence of these organizations. They aspire to become noted for their findings and scientific advancements and achieve this by actively recruiting the best scientists and scholars—those known for their expertise as demonstrated through the recognition of their research and publications. Upon becoming a member of this community, one is expected to make continued contributions to the advancement of knowledge. Members are promoted based on their ability to actively pursue and advance new theories, ideas, concepts, and technologies.[24]

The achievement culture's pathway to success is through the recruitment of the brightest and most talented people who will contribute to a performance level that makes it superior to others. The achievement culture aspires to be the best; to win clients and customers by offering products, services, processes, or technologies that are unequaled in the marketplace. They believe that superiority in quality and service dominates in a competitive market.

Members of this culture value intelligence, ingenuity, and innovation.

The achievement culture is a high-energy culture in which individuals constantly seek to make breakthrough findings and discoveries. The goal is to maximize output and potential by being the best, being first, and being unique.[25]

The achievement culture thrives on knowledge and information. The more new knowledge it gains, the more superior it feels toward other organizations in its competitive domain. These organizations rely heavily on research and development as the method to gaining superiority over others. Experts and professionals are drawn to the achievement culture because achieving technical ideals and gaining preeminence motivate them.

Who you know or how personable you are has nothing to do with getting ahead in the achievement culture. Merit is the primary criterion that wins the respect of colleagues and superiors. You earn this confidence and respect by what you contribute and what you achieve. People who "talk" a good game do not last very long in the achievement culture. This logical culture is void of emotion and pomp and circumstance. The important virtue is demonstrated performance and proven accomplishment.

The emphasis of the achievement culture is to do or be the best. Since being the best is tied to superiority, members are encouraged and even compelled to put forth their best effort. Significant accomplishments are simply plateaus or standards to surpass. This is a "continuous improvement" culture that focuses on its weaknesses and downplays its strengths. People in this culture possess a sense of urgency because something always has to be improved upon or discovered. To let down their guard is to give the competition an opportunity to outdo them in some area. Celebrating or feeling satisfied about a particular accomplishment is shunned by the achievement culture. It doesn't rest long on its laurels and has the discipline to drive on to new heights and accomplish even more. The achievement culture thrives on challenge and competition. It enjoys being given a challenge or being told "It can't be done." Individuals in this culture will work relentlessly to prove otherwise.

The achievement culture is comprehensive and thorough. It takes pride in analyzing problems in depth, doing the job in an exhaustive manner, and following through with thoroughness. No stone is left unturned, and there is no shooting from the hip. The toughest problems are dealt with carefully. Claims and assumptions must be backed by data, logic, and fact. The achievement culture is attracted to problem solving as it is to competition. Taking on complex problems is inherently enjoyable to its members who love the challenges that test their talents and capabilities.

THE CONSISTENT CULTURE

The *consistent* cultural pattern emanates from military/police organizations. The leadership of a consistent organization values predictability and order. It strives to consistently produce key results expected by its various stakeholders. It monitors results versus plan in some detail, identifying deviations, and then planning and organizing to resolve these deviations.[26]

Consistent cultures abhor randomness. A consistent culture establishes detailed steps and timetables for achieving needed results and then allocating the resources necessary to make that happen. It establishes structure for accomplishing plan requirements and provides policies and procedures to help guide people, and creates systems to monitor implementation.

The consistent culture doesn't like surprises, especially unpleasant ones. Diagnostic control systems are used to ensure that important goals are being achieved efficiently and effectively. These control systems also allow the leadership to focus on strategic uncertainties, to learn about threats and opportunities as external conditions change, and to respond proactively.

Members are encouraged to initiate process improvements and new ways of responding to customers' needs—but in a controlled way. The consistent culture believes that members should not be given a blank check to do whatever they please. Boundary systems establish the rules of the game and identify actions and pitfalls that members must avoid. These boundary systems are established not necessarily to tell members what to do, but to tell them what not to do. This allows innovation, but within clearly defined limits. The boundaries are set by standards of behavior and codes of conduct and are written in terms of activities which are off limits. They are the consistent culture's brakes.[27]

The consistent culture prizes objectivity. Subjectivity and "soft" concepts are viewed with a jaundiced eye. Empiricism and the systematic examination of externally generated facts are highly valued. Consistent culture leaders are strong skeptics. They want evidence and proof of everything.

The consistent culture is a highly structured environment. Standardization and routinization are valued. Leaders use tools such as profit plans, budgeting, goals, and objectives as a means for guiding and monitoring the performance of the enterprise. Goals common to the entire organization are established. These goals are quantifiable and measurable. A feedback system is put in place to provide opportunities to make improvements. All forms of waste are identified, examined, and reduced. Processes are used to ensure that standards are met in areas such as quality, customer satisfaction, and on-time delivery. These processes are automatically audited to ensure conformance to established standards. Documentation exists for all products and processes.[28]

Neatness and orderliness are clearly visible in a consistent culture. Workplaces are neatly arranged. Organizational documents such as organization charts, policies, and procedures are regularly updated. Meetings have planned agendas, work is planned in advance, and roles and responsibilities are clearly delineated. Messy, disorderly conditions do not exist in a consistent culture.

The consistent culture also values stability. Its organization is usually a hierarchical structure with associated characteristics as a clear chain of command, vertical information flow, linear planning, well-defined functions, and efficient processes. Clear direction and productive outcomes are very important. Economically realistic objectives, data analyses, logical decisions, controlled action, and measured success are also key elements of this culture.[29]

CULTURE FUNCTIONING

Every organization has a purpose or mission. In fulfilling its mission, an organization must think and decide what specific initiatives it will pursue and what actions it will take. The way that it thinks and decides will be very much influenced by the positive elements it adopts from each of the four cultural patterns previously described. The positive core elements of the four cultural patterns can be represented by a horizontal and vertical axis. The horizontal axis expresses a personal versus logical orientation. The personal side reflects a strong orientation toward a concern for people as human beings. The two cultural patterns that have a personal orientation are *cooperation* and *inspiration*. The logical side includes elements that stress impersonal, critical, and analytical thinking—the two cultural patterns that have a logical orientation are the *achievement* and *consistent*.[30]

The vertical axis represents a time perspective of reality versus vision. Reality represents the here and now—it includes the two cultural patterns of *cooperation* and *consistent*. The vision side includes the cultural patterns of *inspiration* and *achievement*. They have a strong orientation toward the future.

Figure 2.2 shows that cooperation and consistent contain elements that focus on the present; that inspiration and achievement elements are future-oriented; that cooperation and inspiration contain elements that value personal concerns; and that consistent and achievement elements value logical thought. Each cultural pattern, then, combines the positive elements from the horizontal-vertical model so that cooperation becomes a reality-personal cultural pattern; inspiration becomes a vision-personal cultural pattern; achievement becomes a vision-logical cultural pattern; and consistent becomes a reality-logical cultural pattern.

PERSONAL ORIENTATION ELEMENTS

As Figure 2.2 indicates, each cultural pattern has a personal orientation that is influenced by its emphasis on personal versus logical concerns. Elements in each of the four cultural patterns stress either analytical, logical problem solving or compassionate, person-centered values. Logical analysis elements involve the use of detached cause-and-effect reasoning. Per-

Figure 2.2
Cultural Pattern Elements

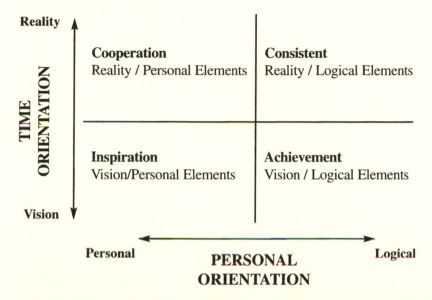

sonal and people-centered elements consider what is important to those affected by decisions. These elements value harmony and recognition of individuals.

The elements of the two logical cultural patterns include the following:

- Value analytical and logical thought
- Stress objectivity and toughness
- Use cause-effect reasoning
- Tend to be task-oriented
- Strive for impersonal, objective truth
- Function with reasonableness
- Stress fairness

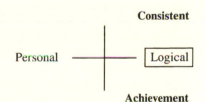

Elements of the logical cultural patterns stress the logical consequences of a choice or action. The aim is to be objective and analyze cause and effect. Consistent and achievement, both logical cultural patterns, use documentation, systems, procedures, and rules so people can make logical, objective decisions every day, not just once in a while. In the consistent culture, people are provided with a methodology that achieves and enhances predictability. It stresses objective standards and requires objectivity and application of principles. It designs and implements rules and procedures. The achievement culture inspires pursuit of extraordinary standards and goals. Scientific methods are used with the objective standard of truth and empirical principles being employed. Consistent and achievement elements emphasize rational reasoning and logic.

The elements of the two personal cultural patterns include the following:

- Tend to be humanistic
- Value kindness and generosity
- Guided very much by ethics
- Tend to be tactful and cooperative
- Strive for harmony and individual validation
- Tend to be friendly and cheerful
- Show concern for the welfare of others

Cooperation

Personal ——— Logical

Inspiration

Elements of the personal cultural pattern stress the importance of individuals working together, sharing responsibility, and helping one another grow and develop. Cooperation and inspiration cultures place much emphasis on personal growth and development. The thinking is that people grow and develop by taking on shared responsibilities, solving problems through discussions of feelings and interactions with others. The focus for both cultural patterns is on nurturing or uplifting one another and fellow human beings to higher levels of competence, dignity, and personal pride. In the cooperation culture, this is accomplished through teamwork. In the inspiration culture, it is accomplished through empowerment. Cooperation and inspiration elements emphasize caring, compassion, and harmony.

TIME-ORIENTATION ELEMENTS

The other major factor influencing the four cultural patterns is time orientation. Each has positive elements that focus either on what is real or what is possible. Reality has to do with what is; vision has to do with what might be. The elements of reality cultures focus on actual concrete experience and reality. The elements of vision cultures focus on future possibilities.

The elements of the two reality cultural patterns include the following:

- Focus on the environment and its demands
- Value realistic and practical applications
- Tend to be factual and concrete
- Focus on the present
- Rely on observable and measurable data
- Approach issues systematically and in orderly fashion
- Trust the past and value experience

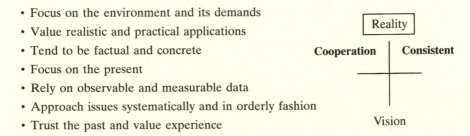

Reality

Cooperation | **Consistent**

Vision

Consistent and cooperation reality cultural patterns are focused on doing what needs to be completed today. Consistency is based on what is, not what might be. The consistent culture stresses stability and control. The major concern is with stability, permanence, and efficient, smooth operations. The cooperation culture focuses on cohesion and trust among constituents. Team work and cooperation needs attention now, not in the future. The problems and concerns of the organization must be addressed now in a team effort. The emphasis is on teamwork, participation, and consensus. Both consistent and cooperation cultures are highly practical (i.e., they are results-oriented and are focused on everyday matters).

The elements of the two vision cultural patterns include the following:

- Look beyond the present into the future
- Value intuition and imagination
- Tend to be abstract-and idea-oriented
- Seek patterns and meaning in facts
- Be lively, animated, and spontaneous
- Tend to be flexible and unstructured
- Be optimistic about future possibilities

Inspiration and achievement, the vision cultural patterns, contain elements that are focused on looking to and planning for the future. The emphasis is to look forward to possibilities of the future. The achievement culture focuses on beating the competition, risk taking, experimentation, and innovation. The focus is on being on the leading edge. Long-term emphasis is on growth and acquiring new resources. The inspiration culture emphasizes flexibility and individuality. Humanism is highly valued. Both cultures are centered on curiosity and creativity and are engaged in exploring the future. For inspiration and achievement, life lies beyond the immediate and into a bigger and brighter future.

This model, as with other similar culture models, is closely linked to the Jungian conceptual dimensions of perceiving and judging functions. These dimensions can be measured using the Myers-Briggs Type Indicator (MBTI) Personality Inventory.[31] The Jungian theory and the application of the MBTI to this model are explained in Chapter 5.

3

The L⁴ Organization—
Adaptive and Consistent in
Achieving Success

If you had your choice, which one of the four cultural patterns would you like to adopt for your organization? The *inspiration* culture? The *achievement* culture? The *cooperation* culture? Or the *consistent* culture? Choosing one cultural pattern assumes that it is superior to the others. That assumption is obviously flawed, because each of the four cultural patterns has positive elements which are beneficial to an organization's success. The L⁴ strategy recognizes this and strives to incorporate the positive elements of all four cultural patterns to establish the L⁴ organization. The L⁴ organization is balanced, complete, and integrated. Adopting just one cultural pattern is an L¹ strategy. The power of the positive elements of one cultural pattern is influencing the organization, but the potential for even greater positive power is limited because the positive elements of the other three cultural patterns are not present and functioning within the organization.

The L⁴ strategy calls for leadership initiatives that move the organization toward balanced integrity. This enables the organization to strengthen its performance, become more adaptive, and sustain successful performance and growth in the midst of changing external conditions (competition, governmental regulations, economic conditions, and emerging technologies). Some organizations adopt one or two cultural patterns to respond to the existing external conditions. This strategy may be effective in the short term; but when external conditions change, these organizations try to adapt but they find themselves ill prepared to redefine themselves and adapt to the new conditions. They achieve success as unbalanced, incomplete organizations, which validates their assumptions that an unbalanced, incomplete organization can succeed.[1] I will discuss these unbalanced, in-

Figure 3.1
The L⁴ Organization

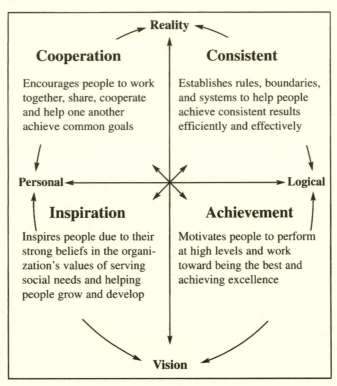

complete organizations in a later chapter; but for now, let us look more closely at the model of an L⁴ organization.

The L⁴ organization has an integrated and balanced culture. As stated previously, the culture is said to be integrated when positive elements complement, not oppose one another. The culture is balanced in the sense that positive elements are in place and functioning, and no set of elements is dominating over others.

Figure 3.1 graphically represents the balance and integration of the positive elements that form the L⁴ organization. It shows that the performance of an organization can be increased by adopting the important positive elements of all four cultural patterns. This is a "meaningful whole" or "complete" organization. Such an organization is close to symmetry. Healthy patterns of complementary, positive elements are in place; unhealthy patterns of negative elements are absent.[2] There is balance within the organization, balance between what appears to be opposing forces. For example, this organization faces the reality of the current situation but also anticipates future trends. It focuses on what needs attention now but doesn't overlook the need to plan long-range goals. It stands for human-centered values, but it doesn't overlook the need to implement methods and systems so it can operate efficiently and effectively.

TWO MAJOR FINDINGS

Here are two major findings I have discovered as a result of my consulting work and research in this area of leadership and culture formation.

Finding One. Organizations that strive to achieve integrated and balanced cultures are more successful, more adaptive, and thus better able to sustain their success over longer time periods than organizations whose cultures are incomplete and out of balance.

Finding Two. Leaders (i.e., executives, managers, and supervisors) of less successful organizations that have incomplete and unbalanced cultures are skeptical about Finding One. They believe other organizations are more successful than they are for other reasons such as better technology, superior equipment, more talented people, more resources, more capacity, and the like. Trying to convince them otherwise is a challenging task. An even more formidable task is trying to convince those in an incomplete, out-of-balance culture that is currently successful that this success may be short-lived unless they strive to form a more integrated, balanced culture.

To strengthen my argument, I like to point to organizations that have achieved long-term success in a challenging industry. The industry that best illustrates this is the information-technology industry. This is an industry that is best characterized by turbulent change—accelerated growth, new and fierce competition, and rapidly changing technology. Surviving and succeeding in this dynamic environment requires adaptability and nimbleness of the highest order. A quick lesson you learn in this industry is this: if you begin a decline, it is very difficult to recover. You may be riding the wave of greatness one day, and the next day you may find your organization is fodder for the obituary column of the business section.

Many who have started in this industry are either out of business or struggling to stay in business, but take a close look at the ones who have succeeded. They have done well, very well, according to financial performance indicators. Their success is documented in the financial presses such as *BusinessWeek* and the *Wall Street Journal*. There is a particular group of top performers who have earned straight As for their financial performance for the past one-, three-, five-, and ten-year periods. In other words, the performances of these companies are not flukes or aberrations.[3] As a matter of fact, even the blue-chip firms that are favorites among business leaders have not performed as well and consistently as these companies. They demonstrate consistent patterns of success and growth which bode well for their future prospects; and one of the major reasons for their continued success is the balanced, integrated cultures formed by the leaders of these organizations. I call them companies of the future not only because of their bright future prospects, but also because they serve as models for other companies to emulate in how to work toward forming an integrated and balanced culture.

Among the top performers who fall into this category are Compaq Computer, Intel, and Hewlett-Packard. Here are some highlights about each of these organizations and their cultures to demonstrate the completeness, balance, and adaptiveness that have been built into the fabric of these successful companies.[4]

COMPAQ COMPUTER

Compaq was founded in 1982 and is the world's largest supplier of desktop and portable personal computers as well as powerful servers that support business applications. Compaq built the first IBM-compatible, portable computer. It was the first computer company to introduce a worldwide, three-year warranty and service program. It attained *Fortune* 500 ranking and reached $1 billion in sales faster than any other U.S. company. Compaq has been recognized as one of the 100 best companies to work for in America, and it has enjoyed consistent market share and financial growth for well over a decade. Today, Compaq is the number one PC provider in the world, and it is ranked fifth in the world in computer sales.[5]

That story may sound like smooth sailing straight to the top, but that was not the case. During 1991 Compaq almost went under. Stiff competition was provided by companies such as Dell Computer, which could thrive on much lower margins than Compaq. As a result, Compaq suffered several quarters of financial losses and falling market share. Compaq had to radically change if it was to survive, and it did. The leadership of Eckhard Pfeiffer and the strength and adaptiveness of Compaq's culture allowed it to turn the situation around and remain a leading player in the computer market. The qualities that helped turn the company around are still in place today—dedication, value pricing, excellent performance, high quality, unmatched reliability, and an unparalleled commitment to superior customer service.[6]

Here is Compaq's company vision: "Compaq, along with our partners, will deliver compelling products and services of the highest quality that will transform computing into an intuitive experience that extends human capability on all planes—communication, education, work, and play."[7]

This vision statement sets the tone for a well-balanced, integrated culture. It alludes to cooperation in understanding and meeting the needs of partners—internal (fellow employees), business partners, and external customers. It inspires its members to fulfill the worthy cause of extending human capability. It sets the lofty achievement of transforming computing into an intuitive experience. It implies the need for consistency in order to deliver compelling products and services of the highest quality.

Cooperation and inspiration have been evident throughout the history of the company. It continues to recruit and develop talented and diverse people. It empowers individuals to become part of teams and fosters an environment of dignity, integrity, and inclusion, one in which all employees are valued and respected. In the Houston area, where more than 10,000 Compaq employees live and work, community involvement is clearly a commitment. Compaq and its employees are actively involved in community activities in areas of education, health, social services, and the arts. In addition to all this, Compaq continually reviews product designs, manufacturing processes, materials, recycling, and treatment technologies to ensure it is protecting the environment and the communities where it operates.

Compaq's past achievements are quite impressive, but it does not rest on its laurels. Its future goal is to become the computer industry's undisputed worldwide leader in customer satisfaction. Another ambitious goal for Compaq is to be the top global computer company by the year 2000.

Compaq realizes the importance of maintaining consistency in quality of product and service, especially now that its products and services are sold in over 100 countries. In its quest to ensure consistency, it recently appointed a vice president of quality and customer satisfaction. It plans to implement a number of initiatives through a corporate-wide quality-management process to achieve its commitment toward the highest levels of quality, customer satisfaction, and brand loyalty.

Compaq offers an excellent example of how value statements can set the stage for organizational actions and behaviors. The culture of Compaq is reflective of the L⁴ model and demonstrates how an integrated and balanced culture can contribute to organizational effectiveness.

INTEL

In 1971, Intel introduced the world's first microprocessor, which sparked a computer revolution that has changed the world. About 75% of the personal computers in use around the world today are based on Intel architecture microprocessors. Today Intel supplies the personal computer industry with the chips, boards, systems, and software that are the "ingredients" of the most popular computing architecture. These products help create advanced computing systems for personal computer use.[8]

When Gordon Moore and Robert Noyce founded Intel in 1968, they knew the kind of company environment they did not want to create. They both came from Fairchild Semiconductors, which had a company environment they considered to be stifling because of its hierarchical business structure. Both wanted to create a company that was void of a social hierarchy, one that had no executive suites, no pinstripe set, no reserved parking places, or other artifacts of the hierarchy.

They viewed their new company as a community of individuals with common interests that had come together in a cooperative venture. Noyce and Moore founded Intel with a plan to exploit LSI, a fast-emerging technology that placed thousands of microminiature electronic devices on tiny silicon chips. Their plan was to supplant core memory, the dominant computer storage technology at the time, with semiconductor memory, an unproven technology. Developing a whole new product category required an environment in which people worked together as a team, designing and building chips with extremely precise detail which necessitated a disciplined, attention-to-detail work style and a strong-willed attitude of staying at the forefront of what would become an extremely competitive, high-technology industry. While the Intel culture has changed slightly over time, most of the principles that the founders built into the company from day one are still an integrated part of a balanced culture, as illustrated by the following value statements.[9]

Cooperation

- "Listen to all ideas and viewpoints."
- "Listen to our partners well."
- "Communicate mutual intentions and expectations."
- "Make it easy to work with us."
- "Work as a team with respect and trust for each other."
- "Be open and direct."

Inspiration

- "Encourage and reward informed risk taking."
- "Learn from our successes and mistakes."
- "Be an asset to the community."
- "Have fun!"
- "Continuously learn, develop, and improve."
- "Take pride in our work."

Achievement

- "Embrace change."
- "Challenge the status quo."
- "Deliver innovative and competitive products and services."
- "Set challenging goals."
- "Execute flawlessly."

- "Focus on output."
- "Assume responsibility."
- "Confront and solve problems."
- "Recognize and reward accomplishments."

Consistent

- "Manage performance fairly and firmly."
- "Maintain a safe and neat workplace."
- "Do the right things right."
- "Practice Intel basics."
- "Conduct business with uncompromising integrity and professionalism."
- "Clearly communicate intentions and expectations."
- "Make and meet commitments."
- "Properly plan, fund, and staff projects."
- "Pay attention to detail."

These value statements may appear to be corporate public relations rhetoric, but nothing could be further from the truth. These values became more deeply embedded as the company grew from a maker of chips into an industry leader (Intel microprocessors power more than 75% of all the PCs in the world). This has all come about through visionary leadership and an organizational leadership strategy aimed at forming a balanced and adaptive culture required to sustain an aggressive growth strategy.

Around 1990, CEO Andrew Grove accelerated the company's plan to become an industry leader. It was then that Intel recognized a major problem for the company. The speed of the microprocessor was starting to outpace the rest of the PC machinery. The internal network, called the "bus" that directs electrons around the computer, would serve data at a rate lower than the Intel Pentium chip would be able to handle. Buyers of computers would therefore not get the power of the Pentium chip and would be disappointed. The design of these buses, until then, came from PC makers such as IBM. Intel's bold decision to design buses led to Intel's PCI which is now the standard bus on PCs.[10]

Craig Barrett, the recently named CEO to succeed Grove, was at one time Intel's quality-assurance program manager. He is credited with designing and managing memory chip manufacturing operations (called "fabs") that are more efficient than any of its competitors. This has allowed Intel to increase microprocessor power while decreasing costs. Intel has had a phenomenal growth period and, according to Barrett, must now make Intel's existing fabs even more productive and efficient.[11]

The above *achievement* and *consistent* cultural characteristics are balanced with *cooperation* and *inspiration* characteristics. Intel's work environment fosters trust and cooperation within its work force. It also has established partnerships with other companies in trying to stimulate demand for PCs. Rather than favor one company over another (e.g., Netscape and Microsoft), Intel will work closely with each in establishing an open framework so everyone can have the opportunity to compete and innovate.

Intel has not lost its inspiration qualities; in fact, it has intensified. Intel continues to increase its dedication to being a responsible corporate citizen. It constantly promotes public understanding of technology and strives to improve the quality of life in the communities in which employees live and work. A major focus of its outreach and giving programs is on education, learning, and technology literacy programs. Intel places a special emphasis on the support of schools, specifically in math, science, and engineering education. Through the "Intel Involved" program, employees serve as volunteers to schools and nonprofit organizations in all Intel site communities. The key to Intel's continued growth and success is for the entire industry to keep expanding. Any hiccup in growth of the PC industry can be a threat to Intel. To maintain Intel's growth, it recognizes the need to devise a strategy that will keep it moving in the right direction while maintaining its balanced and adaptive culture.

HEWLETT-PACKARD

Hewlett-Packard (HP) is probably the oldest existing high-technology company that has demonstrated characteristics of the L^4 model in its early stages and continues to evolve toward integration and balance today. The well-known history of HP began in 1939 when Bill Hewlett and Dave Packard started Hewlett-Packard out of Packard's garage. They started with a philosophy which was formalized into the "HP way" and was stated in written corporate objectives in 1957.[12] Today, the HP way is communicated through the company's statements on organizational values, strategies, and practices. These values and practices demonstrate the integration and balance HP continues to pursue and are illustrated by the following management principles.[13]

Cooperation

- "HP people contribute enthusiastically and share in the success that they make possible."
- "We expect HP people to be open and honest in their dealings to earn the trust and loyalty of others."
- "We achieve our common objectives through teamwork."

- "We recognize that it is only through effective cooperation within and among organizations that we can achieve our goals."
- "Our commitment is to work as a worldwide team to fulfill the expectations of our customers, shareholders, and others who depend on us."
- "The benefits and obligations of doing business are shared among all HP people."

Inspiration

- "We have trust and respect for individuals."
- "We approach each situation with the belief that people want to do a good job and will do so, given the proper tools and support."
- "We conduct our business with uncompromising integrity."
- "Trust and respect for individuals are apparent when MBWA (management by wandering around) is used to recognize employees' concerns and ideas."
- "Trust and integrity are important parts of the open-door policy."
- "HP people shall personally accept responsibility and be encouraged to upgrade their skills and capabilities through ongoing training and development."

Achievement

- "We encourage flexibility and innovation."
- "We attract highly capable, diverse, innovative people and recognize their efforts and contributions."
- "We focus on a high level of achievement and contribution."
- "Our customers expect HP products and services to be of the highest quality and to provide lasting value. To achieve this, all HP people, especially managers, must be leaders who generate enthusiasm and respond with extra effort to meet customer needs."
- "For us to remain in the forefront in all our activities, people should always be looking for new and better ways to work."

Consistent

- "Management by objective: Individuals at each level contribute to company goals by developing objectives which are integrated with their managers' and those of other parts of HP."
- "Written plans guide and create accountability throughout the organization."
- "We strive for overall objectives which are clearly stated and agreed upon, and allow people flexibility in working toward goals in ways that they help determine are best for the organization."
- "Management by objectives is reflected in cooperative and complementary efforts, and cross-organizational integration."

Hewlett-Packard has had a remarkable history of successful performance and growth. It has been selected to be among *Fortune*'s ten most admired companies in 1998.[14] HP, which is well-known for electronic devices and computer accessories (laser and ink-jet printers), has forged into the consumer PC market, and the results are impressive. HP has moved from the world's eleventh largest maker of personal computers to the number three position. It is now targeting the $40 billion photography market with a line of digital cameras, photo scanners, and photo printers.

Twenty years ago HP was in the business of making scientific instruments like spectrometers. Currently, it is more of a computer company. It could someday become a highly successful photography company.[15] The flexibility and adaptability of its L^4-type culture enables it to respond to changing markets and approach change as a constant series of opportunities.

FURTHER EVIDENCE

In the book *Corporate Culture and Performance*, authors John Kotter and James Heskett show the results of their comprehensive analysis of how the culture of a corporation powerfully influences its economic performance. They analyzed more than 200 companies. The authors describe how shared values and unwritten rules can profoundly enhance economic success or conversely lead to failure to adapt to changing markets and environments. One of the major conclusions of their study was that firms cannot adapt if they have unhealthy (unbalanced) cultures and, therefore, will not promote superior performance over long periods of time.[16]

Working with the ideas of Kotter and Heskett, the IBM Consulting Group conducted a benchmark study of 37 *Fortune* 500 companies from 1993 to 1995 and found that a company's culture directly impacts its information technology (IT) performance. What they found was that the more versatile or adaptive an IT organization's culture was, the better it performed in the 22 key management processes they studied. Those processes included developing architectures, migrating legacy systems, measuring the business value of projects, and supporting business with IT plans. They defined adaptive culture as the following (corresponding L^4 cultural patterns are indicated in parentheses):[17]

- Vision and values positively affect behavior. (Inspiration)
- Employees have confidence in the organization's leadership. (Inspiration)
- A focus exists on stakeholders, such as customers and employees. (Cooperation)
- Innovation and appropriate risk taking are encouraged. (Achievement)
- An external focus is kept on competition. (Consistent)

They found that these values and behaviors are noticeably absent from organizations with a change-resistant culture. They conducted a scatter-gram which yielded a positive correlation between adaptive culture and process performance. In their conclusion, they urge companies to develop an adaptive culture because it is well worth the time and effort.

OTHER EXAMPLES

Two well-known companies that have transformed themselves, utilizing approaches which reflect the L⁴ strategy, include the Chrysler Corporation and IBM. Chrysler Corporation was selected as the "Forbes Company of the Year" in 1996. Its turnaround performance is an example of the fact that you do not have to be in a growth industry to succeed in utilizing actions which reflect the L⁴ strategy. Chrysler finished 1996 returning five dollars a share on $60 billion in sales. The return on net sales was above 6%—impressive for a car manufacturer. GM has been running only 4%; Ford, a bit under 3%. The average for all 1,280 companies covered by Forbes for 1996 was 4.6%.[18]

Chrysler's return on capital was 20%—again very impressive for a company in a capital-intensive business. The all-industry median was 9.6%; the auto and truck industry median was 8.2%. One in every six vehicles sold in America in 1996 was a Chrysler, up from seven the previous year. At this writing, the company has merged with Daimler-Benz AG, the German car manufacturer famous for its luxury car, the Mercedes Benz. The new company, Daimler Chrysler AG, is now the world's third-largest car maker.

That is a dramatic change for a company that was experiencing major difficulties in the early 1990s. Back then, Chrysler had terrible customer service and press relations with a history of innovation but a present of outdated products. Its market share was falling, and its fixed costs and losses were high.[19] Bob Lutz, the president, wanted Chrysler to become the technology and quality leader in cars and trucks—a clear, globally applicable vision. A program of culture change was built around it. Following are some of the initiatives credited with changing the way the company did business using the same people. These major initiatives reflect the formation of a balanced, integrated culture similar to the L⁴ model.[20]

Cooperation

Characteristic of the "new" Chrysler is the platform team, a Chrysler creation. A team of engineers, designers, suppliers, and factory workers is created around each vehicle platform. They work together simultaneously. In the old system, each functional group did its work and passed it on to the next group. The platform team means speed and reduced costs. For example, the new Durango utility vehicle took only 24 months to build, about as short a time as anyone in the world creates a vehicle.

Another cooperative effort is the supplier relationship. It is not just beating on suppliers to cut prices; it involves bringing them in early as partners with the platform team. One of the reasons Chrysler product development costs are so low (2.7% of revenues, half the competitions) is that suppliers do much of the work.

Inspiration

Most people like building a quality product. It's natural to want one's labors to produce something of quality and beauty. Workers will believe in and support quality efforts if they see them as being sincere. Chrysler has been very sincere and committed to quality through its quality initiatives.

Involvement, empowerment, and learning are also characteristics of the new Chrysler culture. Factory workers are now involved in the design teams. Learning and self-development occur as these individuals directly interact with other professionals in analyzing and solving problems at the platform team level. Achievements and mistakes of one team are shared with other teams which may be facing similar problems. This sharing of information throughout the teams helps to create a learning culture and increase the number of improvements made each year.

Achievement

Driving to excel and be the best in an industry requires champions that promote excellent performance. Chrysler had a lot of them throughout its management ranks. Here are some comments about key players at Chrysler who helped create an achievement-oriented culture.

- Francois Castaing, a Frenchman who built race cars for Renault, was chief engineer at Chrysler. He created the revolutionary platform team.
- Thomas Gale was the designer who created the Chrysler look with the wheels pushed out to the edges, creating extra room inside. His desire was to make Chrysler products to be "remarkable."
- Thomas Stallkamp, who turned parts buying into a major strategic initiative, is a key to the Chrysler success. His efforts resulted in saving Chrysler over $4 billion from 1995 to 1998.
- Dennis Pawley, a GM and Mazda veteran, headed manufacturing and insisted his Chrysler operating system would be superior to Toyota's. He continually squeezed out more production without building more factories.
- James Holden was in charge of marketing. He followed through on plans to cut thousands of dollars per vehicle spent on distribution.

- Theodore Cunningham took over the Mexican operation when the economy there collapsed. Cunningham has the Mexico operation running at a profit as of this writing, and that means the domestic operation there, excluding the profits on the vehicles exported to the United States. He plans to increase the Mexican business again, excluding exports to the United States up to $20 billion by the year 2000.

The desires and aspirations of these key executives have contributed to the achievement cultural pattern that has helped Chrysler attain its current success. Some have left the newly merged Daimler Chrysler, but their valuable contributions have truly helped transform the former, low-performing Chrysler culture.

Consistent

Chrysler has created systems and processes to ensure that its products continue to meet high-quality standards efficiently and effectively.

In four years, 4,000 ideas have been solicited from suppliers; 60% were used, saving over $235 million. Customers are also called during "virtually every stage" of the development of new models to provide suggestions (rather than just ratings of what they liked). Chrysler has been listening to customers who write to the company, and the designers even respond to some letters by phone. Product teams follow vehicles through their development to identify systems and process issues. These issues are well documented, acted upon, and audited.

In project planning, clearly stated objectives are established from the start. The core objectives must have consensus so that everybody agrees up front and sticks to the plan. There are no last minute changes in focus. Everyone who is involved in setting goals takes personal responsibility for living up to them.

The Chrysler Corporation is positioned to do well moving into the next century. It will be interesting to see how the completed merger between Chrysler and Daimler-Benz will work out. The L⁴ model is an effective tool to evaluate cultural mergers and is covered later in this book.

IBM'S COMEBACK

IBM is back. As indicated by the story in *Business Week*'s June 1, 1998 issue, IBM has become a growth company again. It is gaining new business. Its stock is soaring, and it is regaining the respect of corporate America.[21]

Not long ago, it was regarded as a national disaster, but that image is fast becoming a distant memory. Since taking over, chairman and CEO Louis V. Gerstner, Jr. has been masterminding one of the most remarkable revivals in corporate history: double-digit earnings growth, a laser focus on costs, and one of the industry's most aggressive moves on electronic commerce. Most important, IBM's core business—selling computers and all types of information technology to major corporations—is healthier than it has been in years.

IBM's comeback is due to many things being done right since Louis Gerstner took over in 1992. But it is widely known that the comeback is not due to breakthrough technology, slashing prices, or flashy marketing techniques. From the beginning, Gerstner focused on organizational and management issues and shied away from making fundamental changes in the company's strategies. Under his leadership, IBM is creating an integrated, balanced culture that focuses on customers, learning their needs, and determining how to meet those needs.[22]

The company that had come to be known as distant, arrogant, and unresponsive had transformed itself into a collaborative, partnering company which deals with client-business problems rather than pushing hardware. IBM has hired experts from various businesses and industries to shore up its competencies so it can provide assistance and solutions to industry-specific problems.

Gerstner has reinvented the company with high-performance basic values that have re-engineered its work force. He has taken great strides in placing the right people in the right positions (growing the employee base by approximately 50,000 in a three-year period) and has empowered them to make decisions. He has created a learning environment by insisting that IBM fully exploits networked technologies for employee training. He even takes the opportunity to be the lecturer himself. To deliver more consistent performance, he has instituted systems to lower annual operating costs by $15 billion. This has helped IBM achieve a superior financial performance in recent years. Gerstner pushes for excellence in products and services, which has helped IBM regain its previous positive image with corporations. The company has replaced its aging line of water-cooled mainframes with smaller, faster, and cheaper mainframes. It has improved its personal computer line which has resulted in increased sales. The service area of the company has been drastically overhauled and now provides services and consulting which help bring in even greater revenue than personal computers, and at a higher profit margin. Lou Gerstner's leadership is an excellent example of the power of the L^4 strategy in transforming an organization. His emphasis on core values and leadership actions reflects the positive elements of all four cultural patterns (cooperation, inspiration, achievement, and consistent).

CONCLUDING NOTE

The case studies presented in this section are not, nor are they intended to be, portrayed as scientifically based evidence to conclusively prove the efficacy of the L^4 strategy. As with any practical business application, one first looks at the face validity of a suggested approach (on the surface, does it make sense?) and then attempts to review some supporting examples (has it been successfully applied in the real world of business?). With the examples presented in this section, one can generally conclude that the L^4 strategy offers promise as an organizational leadership strategy in forming a performance-enhancing culture. Conversely, one may ask about the consequences of an organization that is not balanced, but unbalanced. In other words, what is the effect of an unbalanced organization on performance? And are there examples to support the assertions made about unbalanced organizations? This topic is covered in the next chapter.

4

Valuable Lessons from the Unbalanced Organization

There is a principle in the field of psychology that states, "Any positive human trait taken to an extreme can become a weakness." In applying this principle to leadership, consider the quality of "participative" which is broadly defined as "involving subordinates by gaining their input to make informed decisions on important organizational issues." This is generally viewed as a positive leadership quality; however, if this quality is taken to an extreme, it becomes a weakness. In other words, if the leader seeks too much input from subordinates before making every decision, then he/she is viewed as indecisive, wishy-washy, and weak.

The same also can be true of organizations that push too far in implementing the positive elements of just one or two cultural patterns and disregard the positive elements of the others. Pushing too far throws the organization out of balance and makes it susceptible to negative consequences. This overemphasis overplays the positive elements of the cultural pattern(s) being pursued and neglects the important positive elements of the others. The end result is usually sub-par performance, underachievement, and slow or no growth.[1]

What happens in such an overload condition is that positive elements of one cultural pattern are emphasized to such an extreme that these positive elements actually become a weakness in the organization. The organization then operates in an out-of-sync condition, being negatively influenced by the dominance of a lopsided culture.[2] What happens when one cultural pattern is pushed to such an extreme is that the organization becomes culturally out of balance and experiences negative effects, as illustrated in Figure 4.1.

If you work for an organization that has an unbalanced culture, perhaps

Figure 4.1
Negative Effects of an Unbalanced Culture

An overemphasis on:	Results in an organization that is characterized as:
Cooperation	Management by committee; directionless, unaccountable
Inspiration	"Clubby"; soft performance, undisciplined
Achievement	Cold, indifferent, blindly ambitious
Consistent	Controlling, autocratic, political

you can identify with one of the four unbalanced organizations described in the following sections. As examples, I have included some organizations with which I am personally familiar plus larger, national public companies.

THE UNBALANCED COOPERATION CULTURE

The following comments came from a senior manager whom I had known for several years, and who was working for a manufacturing company. The comments reflect his frustration after being with the company for nine months. I valued his opinions because I had known him to be a competent and conscientious manager who got positive results and was well respected within his industry.

In this company, everything is done by committee. The company refers to them as teams. Every time a problem comes up, a team is formed. We have so many teams around here it's hard to keep track. Hell, we got natural work teams, functional teams, project teams, customer teams, product teams—you name it, we got a team for it. This company spends so much time in team meetings, it's a wonder we get anything done around here.

The problem is, we don't seem to be getting very far with these teams. Our quality is still substandard based on our high return rates. Our productivity measures haven't come close to targeted levels consistently for the past three years, and our sales figures have been below projected goals for the past five years. The team concept was implemented here about two years ago, but it hasn't helped this company improve; in fact, things have gotten worse.

Our focus and attention seem to be on "team" rather than on getting results. What we need is strong leadership, not more teams. I'm not sure where this company is headed, nor do a lot of other people around here. We need someone to step up and show us where we are going and tell us how to get there. All this stuff about harmony and teamwork has eliminated any sense of urgency. No one seems to be accountable for getting results. When a problem is brought up, the response is, "The xyz team is working on that."

Don't get me wrong; I'm not against the team concept, but I think we have gone too far. When projects are overdue, deadlines are missed, shipments are late, and no one is held accountable, I think there is a serious flaw in the system. We keep better track of the number of teams and meetings we have than we do of important performance measurements.

This situation is not unique to this company. Thousands of U.S. companies have adopted and fervently embraced the team concept only to be disappointed by the end results. Articles appearing in management journals and the popular business press carry reports of studies that show that team initiatives by U.S. companies are, for the most part, not contributing to significant improvement in organizational performance and results. In fact, some experts estimate that 65% fail to achieve significant measurable results.[3]

Why is this? I contend that a major reason is the following: When a company initiates a major intervention, such as team development, it is usually done with such fervor and zeal that the targeted cultural pattern (in this case, *cooperation*) is emphasized at the expense of the other three. The focus, energy, and attention of the organization is on harmony, teamwork, and cooperation which again are positive organizational attributes; but if pushed too far, they throw the culture out of balance, resulting in negative consequences.

A well-known company was in such a dilemma. Almost everyone knows that Delta Airlines was once the "family" company. It fostered and promoted a family orientation which emphasized the elements of cooperation. As a result, there was a strong family feeling among employees and a loyal bond between management and employees. Delta become known as the "no-layoff" company, even during the hard times of the 1970s and early 1980s. The family feeling among employees extended to customers which helped Delta develop the reputation for offering the highest level of customer service in the industry.[4]

This cooperation cultural pattern emphasis worked well for Delta during the period of industry regulation and stability; but after airline deregulation, Delta faced a totally new environment. With deregulation came new and fierce competition—an environment that Delta had never before faced. Existing and new competitors were fighting for market share by offering lower air fares. All of a sudden Delta, with its unbalanced culture, was facing a price war in which it was unfit to compete. Among its rivals, Delta had the highest operating costs; therefore, to become competitive, it had to reduce fares without suffering significant profit losses.

Faced with this dilemma, the former chairman and CEO, Ronald Allen, moved to counterbalance the culture and enable Delta to survive in its new, fiercely competitive environment. His counterbalance move was stark and drastic. To make Delta more cost-efficient and competitive (moves to *consistent* and *achievement* cultures), he undertook a severe cost-cutting program in 1994 which eliminated 15,000 jobs. This move was unprecedented and unheard of in a company which historically took care of its "family," even in the worst of times.[5]

The counterbalance move was a cultural shock to the organization. Although the move has proven to be financially successful (Delta has the lowest cost of any major airline and has reported consistent quarterly operating profits), the organizational trauma caused low employee morale and diminished customer service. The challenge facing the new president and CEO, Leo Mullin, is to realign the culture for more balance, integrating the positive elements of all four cultural patterns. This must be done in order to restore morale and improve customer service while maintaining its competitive cost advantage.[6]

The Delta situation offers some important lessons. First, it illustrates that an unbalanced culture may function effectively in a certain environment. Second, it shows that when the environment changes, the unbalanced culture is not adaptive in responding to changing environmental conditions. Third, it offers an example of the traumatic effects when severe actions are required to counteract the imbalance; and fourth, it demonstrates the negative aftermath associated with a counterbalance initiative. All of these lessons support the importance of adopting an organizational leadership approach, the L[4] strategy, which is designed to move the organization toward an integrated and balanced culture irrespective of the conditions of the current environment in which it functions.

THE UNBALANCED INSPIRATION CULTURE

A few years ago, a chief operating officer of a suburban community hospital requested my services to help change the culture of his organization. Upon arriving for my first visit, we spent three hours discussing the hospital's current state of affairs. The CEO had been with the organization for eight months. Following are some highlights from that conversation.

Stan, I have been in the health-care business for over 20 years, and I have never seen anything like this place. I guess the best way to describe it is "organized anarchy." On the positive side, it has a very friendly workplace; but on the negative side, it is so lax and so undisciplined that I lie awake at nights worrying about the real possibility of a major "screw-up" involving a patient.

Policies and rules are virtually nonexistent, standard operating procedures are followed sometimes, and performance measurements are foreign to this place. In addition to that, we are overstaffed and undermanaged. We allow the doctors free rein in determining patient care and services, and employees the freedom to determine work schedules and practices. Let me give you an example. Shortly after I arrived on the job, I learned that my executive secretary, who has been here for 18 years, can't take shorthand and doesn't know word processing. After learning this, I went storming down to the HR director to find out how this was possible.

He told me that she was asked repeatedly by the former CEO, Charlie, to enroll in training classes to update her skills; but she made such a fuss that Charlie conceded and allowed her to miss the training classes. This is why we still have a relic IBM typewriter in this organization, and it's in my office area. Well, I got huffy and told the HR director that my secretary would either learn new skills or leave. He responded by advising me to be cautious as no one had been fired from the hospital during his 13 years there; and besides, she was very much liked by the chairman of the board.

I soon found out that this situation was only the tip of the iceberg. This permissiveness is rampant throughout the organization. I found out that people take off whenever they feel like it; departments take two hours to celebrate individuals' birthdays; people come in late and leave early. Besides that, we have the most generous compensation and benefits plan I have ever seen. Listen to this, we pay full coverage for medical and dental insurance; and we reimburse employees 100% tuition for any course they complete whether it's in their field of specialty or not.

This country club atmosphere is a legacy of Charlie, and I am trying to change it with little help from the board of directors. They seem to feel that everything is fine even though we are facing the future threat of a significant financial deficit and the wrath of managed health care around the corner. I need you to help me change this culture and refocus our efforts.

(Note: Shortly after I began to work with the CEO and the organization, the hospital ran into serious financial difficulty and was merged with another institution. It did not survive, nor did the CEO, who was let go just before the merger was completed.)

This is an example of the *inspiration* cultural pattern taken to an extreme. The concern for employees' welfare (i.e., compensation, benefits, development, and accommodating workers) was taken so far that it created an unbalanced situation that ignored the positive elements of the other three cultural patterns, especially *achievement* and *consistent.*

An example of this in the business world is Ben & Jerry's Homemade Inc., the famous maker of ice cream products. The company was founded in 1978 by co-founders Ben R. Cohen and Jerry Greenfield. These two individuals set out to make delicious ice cream and proclaimed, "Let it be a workers' paradise and let it be fun."[7] From this ideal emerged a human resource department that formed and shaped the company's culture. It created a corporate environment that places great value on each employee, rewards workers substantially for their labor, and encourages them to give something of themselves back to their community. It also cheers employees to have fun while they pursue their paychecks.

In 1992, *Personnel Journal* recognized Ben & Jerry's Homemade, Inc. by granting it the Optimas Award in the "Quality of Life" category for creating the supportive environment for employees. It was also recognized for its dedication to social responsibility. This is reflected in its mission, which is to do more than just make ice cream. It also strives to contribute to humankind. The company measures its success by how much it gives back to the community—locally, nationally, and internationally. The corporation makes reference to the dual bottom line of its mission statement: To be profitable for its shareholders *and* to be socially responsible inside and outside the organization.[8]

The company's financial performance was stellar up until 1994. The double-digit earnings for the previous decade made it a favorite among investors; but as sales stagnated at about $150 million in 1994, Ben & Jerry's lost nearly $2 million. The once hot stock fell from a high of 33 to 10. The charismatic co-founder and chairman, Ben Cohen, conceded the company had outgrown his management skills.[9] The company launched a gimmicky search for a CEO with a nationwide essay contest. However, it was a corporate headhunter who helped recruit Robert Holland, a turnaround specialist and onetime McKinsey & Co. consultant, as president and CEO. When Holland arrived, he moved quickly to counterbalance the culture. He took measures to move it more toward the consistent and achievement cultural patterns. He began by instituting tighter controls. For the first time, formal growth plans were being drawn up and budgets were determined. As one company manager stated, "Now, people have numbers they're accountable for."[10]

Product development was equally haphazard and inconsistent. It often depended on what Cohen thought the next flavor should be. To improve product development, Holland expanded the research and development lab. He also recognized manufacturing problems and hired an operations manager with years of experience in food services. The changes paid off. In June 1996, Ben & Jerry's broke its record for weekly sales by 20%, which was attributed to Holland's efforts to introduce a new line of no-fat sorbets launched in March of that year. Sales and earnings improved, and its stock price was trading at 17. Future aggressive growth plans included a move into foreign markets.

Robert Holland served 20 months as CEO. In that very short period of time, he made significant moves to counterbalance the culture and improve its performance. Upon his resignation, Holland stated that Ben & Jerry's was next in need of a strong marketer. In January 1997, the company hired Perry Odak, a marketing specialist, to replace Holland.[11]

In the third quarter of 1997, Ben & Jerry's reported signs of a major turnaround by reporting a 39% jump in net income on 8% higher sales. Odak continued Holland's performance improvements and implemented additional marketing strategies (achievement) by entering new markets, forming new product lines, and bolstering advertising efforts. The more balanced culture of Ben & Jerry's appears to be paying off as the company continues to show earnings gains based on improved performance.[12]

THE UNBALANCED ACHIEVEMENT CULTURE

The positive elements of the achievement cultural pattern provide the driving force for an organization. Achievement elements provide the impetus to improve performance (new or better products/services) and continuous growth (expanding current markets or entering new ones). However, an overemphasis on this cultural pattern can lead to a negative imbalance. Here is an example. I was asked by a longtime friend for some career advice. He was a human resource director for an engineering consulting firm for eight years and was experiencing some difficulty with his job. He described his situation as we talked in his office with the door closed.

Stan, the situation here can best be described as bizarre. We are about to lay off 30% of our work force, and it was only two years ago when I was under the gun by the owners to go out and hire close to 60 engineers and technicians. Back then, the owners had their sites set on growing this organization threefold in five years. They had hired this "hot-shot" sales guy who promised he could make it happen. He was so convincing that the three owners brought him in as an equity partner. This place has not been the same since he joined us.

Shortly after he arrived, I was called in by him and the other owners. They handed me a spec sheet outlining the kinds of engineers and technical people they needed and told me to start hiring as soon as possible. I said, "For what? The business level hasn't increased during the past six months." That's when Mr. Hot Shot spoke up and claimed he had five major contracts in the "pipeline" and reminded me that I shouldn't be questioning a directive from the owners. I was really disappointed in the original three owners for not coming to my support. In fact, I felt like quitting right then and there, but decided to ride it out since the job market was tight for senior HR people like me.

As it turned out, Mr. Hot Shot did land the contracts he claimed to have had. Although he came through, I was still skeptical about this guy. I just didn't trust him. In spite of my concerns, I had to get moving. Start dates were closing fast, and I had a monumental task ahead of me. I spent the next eight months mostly recruiting, interviewing, and hiring people. The load was so great, I had to add another person to my staff to handle the overload.

About a year after this hot-shot guy had arrived, things started going down hill quickly. We learned that Mr. Hot Shot went and low-balled bids to get the jobs. His underbids put us into some serious cost overruns that hurt us financially. We also had a serious cash-flow problem because the contracts he landed required a lot of upfront cost that he didn't mention until after getting the contracts. In addition to all that, we were missing deadlines and mismanaging projects because we were throwing inexperienced engineers in as senior project managers.

Things really got ugly. We were constantly putting out fires. People began to bicker and blame one another for mistakes. The clients were complaining and threatening to withhold payments on completed projects they claimed had to be redone. The major blow that really hurt was the cancellation of two big contracts we were assured of getting by Mr. Hot Shot. He said the contracts were given to other firms because the potential client companies heard about our problems with current contracts. And what about Mr. Hot Shot? Well, he is gone. As soon as he started to see some of the problems of his own creation, he bailed out and smooth-talked his way into another firm.

Now we're trying to put back the pieces and redefine ourselves; but I am not sure we can make it. Employee morale is at an all-time low, and our reputation in the marketplace has been hurt very badly. Our good people have their resumes out on the street; and if we lose them, we definitely won't make it. Things are so bleak that I don't see a future here for me much longer. I thought you might have some ideas on what I should do.

(Note: This firm was never able to recover. The three partners began bickering among themselves as the financial condition of their firm worsened. They were sued by two of their clients over contract disputes and eventually had to file for bankruptcy. My friend became an independent consultant.)

This firm had its sites set on aggressive growth and focused on the achievement cultural pattern. In doing so, it failed to establish the positive elements of the consistent, cooperation, and inspiration cultural patterns. The imbalance produced serious consequences. This is an example of what happens when the direction of the firm is established without an organizational leadership strategy that pursues integration and balance. Another example of this unbalanced approach is demonstrated by a public company in the "for-profit" health-care industry, Columbia/HCA Healthcare Corp.

Columbia/HCA has been recently beset with monumental problems. It has been buffeted by the largest health-care fraud investigation in history. Federal officials have alleged in court documents that the company engaged in a "systematic corporate scheme" to defraud Medicare and other government health insurance funds. The company has denied there was systematic wrongdoing.[13] The problems facing Columbia are the result of an imbalanced culture where emphasis has been focused on the achievement cultural pattern.

HCA and Columbia were two separate companies who joined forces in the for-profit hospital management business. Dr. Thomas F. Frist, Jr., a physician, and his father founded the Hospital Corporation of America (HCA) in 1961 and sold it to Columbia in 1994.[14]

Columbia Hospital Corp. began in 1984 when two individuals, Richard Rainwater and Richard L. Scott, each put in $125,000 to create the company. Their strategy was bold and straightforward: "To establish the company as the lowest-cost, highest-volume health-care provider in as many cities as possible."[15] (Notice the emphasis on achievement here, with no mention of cooperation, inspiration, or consistent cultural elements.)

When the two organizations merged to form Columbia/HCA, Mr. Scott became CEO in 1994 and claimed the chairman's seat in 1996. According to those close to him, Mr. Scott is described as a brilliant entrepreneur with "relentlessly aggressive leadership style." He built a $20 billion, 340-hospital giant through a highly aggressive acquisition strategy. However, in July 1997 he was forced out of office by the board of directors amid the deepening federal investigation. Currently, Dr. Frist is the chief executive of the company.[16] Mr. Scott's strategy and style pushed Columbia's culture into an aggressive growth mode emphasizing an achievement goal of growth while disregarding the positive elements of the cooperative, inspiration, and consistent cultural patterns. According to public reports, here are some of Mr. Scott's actions that helped create the unbalanced achievement culture.[17]

- He had an overly aggressive management style that antagonized regulators, and he set a far too rapid growth strategy.
- He imposed precise and highly ambitious, double-digit revenue and profit goals for his managers.
- He tied managers' compensation to profitability, yet allowed them considerable latitude in running their operations with no monitoring mechanisms in place.
- He formed questionable joint ventures with doctors.
- He bought health-care operations before thoroughly checking them out (many are currently at the center of the Medicare fraud probe).
- He ruled over a weak board of directors who failed to challenge him.

As of this writing, Columbia's future is indeed precarious. It continues to record a flat operating profit resulting from costs related to the criminal investigation into its billing practices and subsequent restructuring actions. Some speculate that it may be sold to a competing organization in the industry. In the meantime, Dr Frist has made moves to fulfill his promise of installing a more open culture.[18]

THE UNBALANCED CONSISTENT CULTURE

Dave, the president of a manufacturing firm in Ohio, called and asked me to come meet and visit with Ralph R., his new vice president of operations. The president wanted me to brief Ralph on the work I had been doing with the company in leadership training and culture development during the six months prior to Ralph's arrival. The president wanted to make sure Ralph was aware of our total company effort to change its culture and improve its performance.

Ralph (who was in his late thirties) had been on the job for five weeks when we met in his office. What struck me immediately about Ralph was his neatness and orderliness. First was his personal appearance. While other managers wore open collar sport shirts and casual pants, Ralph was dressed in a short-sleeve white shirt and tie. He was wearing pleated dress slacks and polished dress shoes. This was not the type of attire I was accustomed to seeing at a manufacturing facility, even among managers. Ralph's office was also extremely neat and orderly. His desk top was essentially bare of papers and folders, having only essential desk accessories (i.e., telephone, clock, in/out basket, calculator). Next to the desk was a computer workstation which was also nicely arranged with neatly stacked and catalogued manuals. His back credenza consisted of only a few items including a framed portrait of his wife and two young children.

After we spent some time getting acquainted, I asked Ralph about his initial impressions of the company. I was surprised by his response. He said he was concerned about the clutter and dirtiness of the factory floor. He expressed that one of his immediate priorities was to "clean up the place." "Clean up the place?" I thought to myself. "This is one of the cleanest and neatest factory shop floors I have seen in years." I changed the topic of conversation by telling Ralph that one of the president's major concerns was to improve relations between management and the workers to create an atmosphere of openness and trust. I pointed out that our leadership training and culture change was focused in that direction.

Ralph responded by telling me that problems between workers and management were due to a lack of control systems. He went on to explain that quality defects and late delivery problems were caused by management's inability to monitor and control worker behavior. "What we need," he said, "are more written standard operating procedures and more written rules on workplace behavior, including written disciplinary procedures." He pointed out, for example, that workers should be disciplined if they do not keep their immediate area clean according to written standards. Another idea he had been thinking about was installing time clocks which would force workers to punch in and out at the beginning and at the end of their work shifts. (The workers were nonunion and had been paid on a salary basis since the company was founded over 30 years ago.)

"Whoa!" I thought to myself. "I had been working here for six months trying to form a balanced culture, and this guy wants to overload consistent elements and throw the organization out of balance." I tried to explain to Ralph that according to my knowledge of the situation, management had to improve communications with the workers and work together in resolving problems relating to quality and late deliveries. Ralph was listening, but I could sense that he was not buying my assessment of the situation, nor my solution.

Following our disappointing meeting, I had to now meet with Dave, the president. He wanted to learn of my impressions of Ralph. Dave was the one who personally recruited Ralph from another company with the help of a headhunter. Dave was really high on Ralph and thought that he was going to be a major asset to the company. During our meeting, I expressed my concerns. I agreed with Dave that Ralph had all the technical skills and knowledge, but I was questioning his management beliefs and whether they fit with the direction we were going with our culture formation. The president reassured me that Ralph was a good man, and that he would work out in the long run.

Eight months later the president called to tell me he had to terminate Ralph. He said that Ralph, as I pointed out, was obsessed with control mechanisms and processes. In addition, his autocratic style of management alienated most of the workers who rebelled against most of his planned changes. The fact of the matter was that quality and delivery problems did not get better; they got worse, and that's when Dave had to pull the plug and let Ralph go. Dave also said that he wanted me to become involved in the search for and selection of Ralph's successor so this wouldn't happen again. Ralph was essentially a command-and-control leader. He came from the big-steel industry where companies are well-known for their overemphasis on the consistent elements and the neglect of the important positive elements of the other three cultural patterns of inspiration, cooperation, and achievement.

Big steel refers to the large, integrated producers of steel which usually include the big six (Armco, Bethlehem, Inland, LTV, National, and USX). At a time not too long ago, these large, integrated steel companies pretty much dominated and controlled the domestic steel market of the United States. In 1979 big-steel companies controlled 78% of the U.S. market; however, today's big six controls less than half.

The cultures of these large steel companies were amazingly similar. Their command-and-control cultures reflected their managements' dominant attitude outwardly as well as inwardly: "This is our product; this is when you will receive it; and if you don't like the price or the quality of what you receive, be our guest and get it somewhere else."

The command-and-control cultures of these big-steel companies were marked by authoritative management, formal rules and policies, many levels of supervision, sharp divisions of labor, and specific work rules. All of this produced companies which had frozen bureaucracies with procedural sterility, trivial rigor, and ironbound traditions. The positive elements of the cooperation, inspiration, and achievement cultures were overshadowed by these command-and-control cultural elements. In the big-steel culture, few decisions were made at the working level, management systems focused on control, there was little information sharing, and employees had little opportunity to influence the course of events in their work areas. Management systems and practices were based on the assumption that employees had little to contribute to the business enterprise.

Then the bottom fell out in the early 1980s. These big-steel companies were all of a sudden facing new and stiff competition. Foreign steel companies from Germany and Japan were importing cheaper and higher grade steel. Domestic mini-mills that recycle scrap steel were stealing market share with cheaper and superior quality; and all this was happening in the midst of weak demand in autos, construction, and other key markets. Massive layoffs occurred at most companies; and in addition, two major producers, LTV Corporation and Wheeling-Pittsburgh Steel Corporation, filed for bankruptcy.[19]

These steel companies established command-and-control cultures so that they could render their business worlds more understandable, predictable, and controllable. This approach worked for a long time because they controlled key markets in a stable business environment. However, when the business environment drastically changed, they found their cultures to be slow in responding and adapting to new business conditions.

Since the mid-1980s these large producers have made major moves to counterbalance their cultures. To become more productive and more competitive (achievement), they have restructured their companies, slashing employment and cutting capacity. They have invested heavily in improving technology by spending millions of dollars in capital improvements. They have focused in improving quality, customer service, and on-time delivery. The managements of these corporations have also focused on instituting teams (cooperation) and providing training and empowering their workers (inspiration).

While the big-steel companies have made major gains as a result of these moves, their cultures are still struggling to change and become more nimble and more responsive to an ever-changing and competitive business environment. Their cultures took a long time to evolve and will take a while to substantively change and become more balanced and adaptive. The big question is whether they can do it in time before the next major downturn in the industry.

COUNTERBALANCE VERSUS REBALANCE MOVE: ASSESSING THE CULTURE

In the previous examples we have seen illustrations of unbalanced cultures and the negative effects they can have on the performance of an organization. In reading about these organizations, you may have noticed that these situations were dire, serious, and in some cases at a crisis stage. The very existence of some of the organizations was in jeopardy. Something stark and dramatic had to be done and done quickly to ensure their survival. In these cases the initiative implemented to save these organizations is what I term a "counterbalance move." A counterbalance move is a severe, radical action or set of actions designed to quickly counteract an existing unbalanced culture. This counterbalance may include actions such as closing plants, replacing leaders, laying off people, selling businesses or instituting tight control systems. This move is usually counter to the culture; it is alien to its belief systems and violates accepted behaviors of the past. Such a radical move is usually a shock to the system. Survivors usually end up in a state of shock, confusion, and disarray. Delta Airlines is a good example. Its severe cost-cutting measure, including the elimination of 15,000 jobs in 1994, was a shock to the system. Its members will take some time to recover from the trauma created by this counterbalance move.

Not all unbalanced organizations require a counterbalance move. In other words, the performance and financial conditions of the organization are not yet at a life-threatening state. Perhaps the organization's performance level is mediocre as is its financial condition. There may be some warning signs of impending dangers, but the organization is not yet in a crisis. In this unbalanced situation, there is time to take a less radical move in correcting the situation. Instead of initiating a counterbalance, the organization may want to initiate a "rebalance move." A rebalance move is completed within a larger time frame because the direction of the unbalance is not yet severe enough to negatively impact performance levels and, consequently, the financial condition of the organization.

How does a leader determine the cultural condition of his/her organization? How is it determined whether the culture is balanced or unbalanced? And further, how does one determine whether a counterbalance or rebalance move is warranted? Actually, the last question requires an answer before the first two questions can be adequately addressed. As pointed out earlier, the decision to counterbalance or rebalance the organization's culture depends upon the performance level and/or the financial condition of the organization. If the performance level and/or financial condition is significantly negative, the organization's culture, in all probability, is severely out of "sync" and will require a counterbalance move—quickly. For example, a company is severely underperforming for six straight quarters and so its board of directors fires the current CEO and brings in an "outsider" as its new leader. The new leader will have to initiate a counterbalance move shortly after arriving in order to offset the unbalance and improve performance quickly.

On the other hand, the performance level and/or financial condition of the organization may be adequate or better; but the organization's culture may also be out of balance. However, the out-of-balance condition may not be as severe as the seriously underperforming organization. This organization may be performing adequately but not to the level of its potential as its leader recognizes. The leader of this organization decides to initiate a rebalance move.

The determination to institute a counterbalance versus a rebalance move is clearly a judgement call on the part of the leader. If the decision is to counterbalance, this initiative calls for a quick assessment of the culture and swift actions to correct the condition. If, on the other hand, the decision is to institute a rebalance move, the cultural assessment and follow-up actions are pursued within a much wider time frame and with much more involvement and participation of the organization's members. This rebalance approach is described later in Chapters 7 and 8.

For the leader who decides to initiate a counterbalance move, the challenges are great, for he/she has only a short time to assess the culture and institute corrective actions to improve the unbalanced condition. An incorrect assessment could result in focusing on the wrong cultural pattern(s) and perhaps worsen an already unbalanced culture which may be the major cause of the organization's underperformance.

Unfortunately, there is no quick, clear-cut method for assessing organizational culture. Most techniques are subjective, open-ended approaches based on a clinical psychology model. This methodology involves the study of an organization's artifacts (e.g., dress code, workplace layout, etc.), espoused values of members (what seems important to members), and underlying assumptions (verification or evidence that espoused values explain behaviors). This approach typically includes a series of discussion meetings and interviews with various groups and individuals to determine the elements of the culture and further, whether one culture or a combination of subcultures are at work driving the behavior of the organization. This elaborate, sophisticated, time-consuming approach is just not practical for a leader who lacks training in organizational behavior. The L^4 model offers a much more structured and less complicated approach. The model presents functional categories (four cultural patterns) which can help the leader conduct the assessment more systematically in a more timely fashion. There are essentially two steps in conducting a cultural assessment using the L^4 model.

The first step is to conduct interviews and discussions with leaders and members of the organization. The purpose of the meeting is to share and discuss the L^4 cultural model. After an explanation, a brief discussion is conducted to ensure that the targeted member(s) fully understands the model. Following this discussion, each member is asked to rate the extent to which the elements of each of the four cultural patterns (cooperation, inspiration, achievement, and consistent) exist within the organization using quantitative responses on a 1 (to a very great extent) to 5 (to a very little extent) scale. Upon rating the organization according to each of the four cultural patterns, the member is asked to offer examples of policies or practices to support each rating.

The second step is to review mechanisms in the organization that verify the cultural patterns reported by members. These mechanisms include organizational design and structure, systems and procedures, and programs and processes. A list of these mechanisms is presented in Chapter 8. The list is helpful in reviewing and classifying mechanisms according to the four cultural patterns. The presence and/or absence of mechanisms tells much about the organization according to the L^4 model.

The leader combines the data and information from steps one and two to determine if there is agreement between the sources. For example, if it is reported by members that the organization overemphasizes teamwork and empowerment (cooperation and consistent cultural patterns), the presence of mechanisms supporting cooperation and inspiration should be present, and the absence of mechanisms supporting consistent and achievement cultural patterns should be apparent. This assessment will help the leader institute a counterbalance move to correct the condition.

The interesting dilemma is who should initiate the counterbalance or rebalance move within the organization. Should it be a leader from the inside or should it be an outsider? The following general rules of thumb are based on past practices that seem to work; but they are not, by any means, presented as fool-proof solutions backed by empirical evidence.

- A counterbalance move usually requires a leader from the outside. It is very difficult for insiders to initiate a radical move that runs counter to the culture that he/she has lived and worked in for a number of years.

- Following the counterbalance move, the next initiative should be a rebalance move to form an integrated, balanced culture. A counterbalance move creates another unbalanced situation which should improve performance and financial conditions in the short term, but will adversely affect the long-term performance and growth of the firm unless corrected.

- Not all leaders can do both. Some are better equipped to initiate counterbalance moves (turnaround specialists). Some are better equipped to initiate rebalance moves (L^4 leaders). Few are equipped to do both. One of the few more well-known leaders who can perform both is Jack Welch of General Electric, who is discussed in a later chapter.

5

On Becoming an L⁴ Leader

How does one become an L⁴ leader? How does one begin shaping a culture for integration and balance in order to achieve successful performance and growth? To address that question, one must explore one's leadership presence. The theories and practices believed to be essential about the proper way to run an organization are manifested, symbolized, or implied in the presence of the leader. The leadership presence is the culminating statement of that person's view of how to lead an organization. Understanding leadership presence more fully requires a definition of what it is and how it is formed.[1]

LEADERSHIP PRESENCE

Leadership presence is often misunderstood to mean things like power, influence, style, and charisma. But leadership presence is not just an abstract concept; it is tangible, palpable, and can be seen and felt. Leaders always possess some semblance of presence, whether they are aware of how it varies or is perceived. I define leadership presence as:

> The living out of knowledge and values in ways such as taking a stand on an issue or by modeling specific behaviors to set an example. By performing these acts, the leader teaches important self-held concepts—that which he/she believes important to the organization's effective performance. These concepts are exuded through the leader's way of being.[2]

Leadership presence is not the same as leadership style which, though an aspect of presence, is not sufficient to define one's leadership essence. Leadership presence is the living out of basic assumptions about how one should influence or lead others. These assumptions can be explicitly displayed or tacitly implied through the leader's presence. Style represents the unique way in which an individual combines such things as voice, gestures, appearance, posture, emotional tone, and general manner. One's style is an important aspect of presence. For example, when one enters a situation and introduces himself or herself, style becomes important in creating presence. However, to concentrate on manner as though it is equivalent to presence is to make the same mistake as valuing form over substance. Unless manner and ideology form a strong, coherent whole, the resulting presence will lack power, especially in affecting the organization's culture.[3]

Summarizing then, leadership style is a more superficial, although important, aspect of presence. Style is the delivery of the message. Style alone cannot account for what is meant when someone says, "Manager Y has a strong presence." Presence denotes an integration of knowledge, values, and behavior. By making behavior an enactment of what the leader knows and believes, presence becomes a powerful force. The deeper the belief and the stronger the delivery, the more powerful the presence; and the more powerful the presence the greater the impact on forming the culture. The question now becomes how to use or develop leadership presence to form a culture of integration and balance.

The development of a leader's presence is heavily influenced by two factors. One has to do with the personal preferences the leader has in cognitive formation and processing;[4] the other has to do with the leadership paradigm he or she relies on in acting out in the role of a leader.[5] Let us explore the first factor of cognitive formation and processing, or one's thinking system.

THINKING SYSTEM

Exploring one's thought-processing system is important because one's assumptions are strongly influenced by the structure of the human consciousness. Swiss psychiatrist Carl Jung developed his theory early in the twentieth century, which states that human beings are born with certain mental and emotional characteristics. Jung believed that although all human beings have capabilities to process information (i.e., to observe, to organize, and to retrieve), there are natural, inborn differences in the way people use these capabilities. Jung's theories have been studied and applied starting with two pioneers, Isabel B. Myers and Katherine Briggs, in the early 1920s. They began developing an instrument to assist people in identifying their own Jungian-type preferences. They eventually developed the Myers-Briggs Type Indicator (MBTI) Personality Inventory. This instrument and theory provides a structured, systematic way of recognizing individual differences and, further, helps understand leaders and how they differ. During the past 20 years, the MBTI has been extensively and effectively used in leadership and management development.[6]

To understand Jung's idea of information-processing preferences, it is instructive to visualize right-or left-mindedness, which people learn to perform physical tasks. Similarly, people have two opposite preferences to perform the mental tasks of gathering information, and structuring and prioritizing the information. Jung described the two opposite preferences for each as follows:[7]

- Perception (gathering information) may be exercised through *sensing* versus *intuition*.
- Judgement (structuring and prioritizing) may be exercised through *thinking* versus *feeling*.

PERCEPTION

People have a preference for gathering information that is either *sensing* or *intuition*. In other words, each individual will have a natural preference for one of these operations. It does not mean that one will be used exclusively in the absence of the other; it simply means one is preferred over the other. Consequently, the non-preferred mental tool will be less developed, less comfortable, and often ignored.

If a leader's preference for gathering information is *sensing*, the focus is on what is actual to the present based on data available to the senses. These leaders tend to be realistic and pragmatic.[8] They have a good grasp of what is actually happening in their organization and like to use factual data in forecasting the future and making decisions. The *sensing* leader will likely be:

- Present-oriented
- Short-term
- Incremental
- Practical
- Tangible
- Reality-based

Those who prefer to gather information through *intuition* like to take in information by seeing the big picture and focusing on the relationship and connection between facts. As leaders, they tend to be visionary and imaginative, have an accurate feel for what is going on, and like to make decisions based on future possibilities they "see." The *intuitive* leader typically is:[9]

- Future-oriented
- Long-term
- Experimental/revolutionary
- Creative
- Intangible
- Visionary

JUDGEMENT

People also have a preference for structuring and prioritizing information that is either *thinking* or *feeling*.[10] Those who prefer *thinking* tend to look at the logical consequences of a choice or action. As leaders, they tend to take a detached, analytical approach to problem solving, to value clarity and accuracy, and to ask tough questions. They typically believe that problems have correct solutions that can be found through analyses, and that these logical, reasonable analyses are the basis for decisions. Thinking leaders are usually:

- Task-oriented
- Tough-minded
- Courageous
- Rational
- Analytical
- Mastery-oriented
- Oriented to problem solving

Those who prefer *feeling* in decision making tend to consider what is important to them and to other people. They mentally place themselves in a situation and identify with the people involved so they can make decisions based on person-centered values. As leaders, they tend to encourage participation and consensus in decision making, and to value and recognize the contributions of others. These leaders are usually:

- Relationship-oriented
- Tender-hearted
- Compassionate
- Interpersonally sensitive

Figure 5.1
Preferences Influencing Leadership Presence According to Jung's Theory

Sensing (S)	
SF Preference:	**ST Preference:**
Focus on practical service to people; tend to be sympathetic, friendly and warm; value personal relationships	Focus on bottom-line realities; tend to be practical, logical, and analytical; value order, structure, and systems
Feeling (F) ———————	——— **Thinking (T)**
NF Preference:	**NT Preference:**
Seek to understand the aspirations of people; tend to be insightful, enthusiastic and value effective communications	Drawn to future possibilities and thrive on developing theoretical concepts; driven to discover new frontiers
Intuition (N)	

- Inspirational
- Value-oriented

Jung also described differences in orientation and direction of energy (extroversion or introversion) and different approaches to structure (judgement or perception). These two dimensions provide additional descriptive information that broadens the preference indicators of one's profile; however, I have found the critical measurements of perception (*sensing* or *intuition*) and judgement (*thinking* and *feeling*) to have greater influence in determining one's preference for a particular cultural pattern. More specifically, it is the combination of these two dimensions that significantly influences one's leadership presence in adopting elements of a particular cultural pattern.

The four possible combinations of perception and judgement are presented and illustrated in Figure 5.1.[11]

- Sensing plus Feeling—SF
- Sensing plus Thinking—ST

Figure 5.2
Cultural Patterns and Jungian Psychological Types

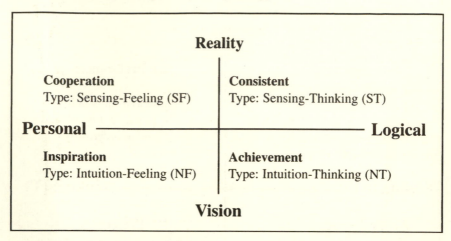

- Intuition plus Feeling—NF
- Intuition plus Thinking—NT

Leaders who are SFs have a daily concern for, and tend to focus on, practical service to people. They are sympathetic, friendly, and warm. A leader with an SF preference will develop a leadership presence that favors the *cooperation* cultural pattern.

Leaders who are NFs seek to understand the aspirations of people. They want to find ways to improve the long-range well-being of all. They tend to be insightful and enthusiastic, and they value effective communications. The NF leader's presence will favor the *inspiration* cultural pattern.

The NT leaders are drawn to future possibilities and thrive on developing theoretical concepts. Their abilities are in analyzing systems and finding ways of improving them. They seek to discover theoretical and technical developments. The NT leader's presence is driven to discover new frontiers and favors the *achievement* cultural pattern.

Leaders who have a ST preference focus on bottom-line realities. They are practical, logical, and analytical. They have developed skills with facts and objects and are drawn to technical concerns. The ST leader's presence strongly values order, structure, and systems, and favors the *consistent* cultural pattern.

The four combinations of SF, NF, NT, and ST illustrated in Figure 5.2 are included within the model of cultural patterns presented in Chapter 2. The presence of type, corresponding to each cultural pattern, illustrates that leaders who favor a particular cultural pattern will develop a leadership presence that will influence the formation of that culture at the expense of others. In other words, leaders have a natural tendency to form an unbalanced culture. The stronger the particular preference, the greater the influence in forming the favored culture, and the more unbalanced the organization becomes. For example, a strongly dominated ST type will tend to be dogmatic and inflexible. This leader will highly value preciseness, orderliness, and systemization. He or she will probably overplan and overmanage. This leader develops elaborate follow-up systems and will strictly follow rules and principles. This leader avoids creative problem solving and forms a culture which is dominated by rules, procedures, and regulations. It is a very restrictive environment in which creativity is not valued and not encouraged. This essentially is the unbalanced *consistent* culture described in Chapter 4.

How does one determine the personal preferences underlying one's leadership presence? There are those with great insight and self-awareness who can identify their personal preferences based on the descriptions provided previously. For those who need help, there is the Myers-Briggs Type Indicator (MBTI) Personality Inventory which was mentioned earlier in this section. The MBTI is one of the most popular self-report instruments used in leadership and management development programs in the United States and around the world. It is designed to provide information about respondents' Jungian psychological type preferences.[12]

LEADERSHIP PARADIGM

Does the previous section suggest that personal preferences will absolutely predict the particular organizational culture a leader will tend to form? Certainly not. It merely infers that the leader will tend to favor one particular cultural pattern, especially if there is no clear mental image of how to otherwise lead others. Stated another way, absent a leadership paradigm, one tends to rely heavily on personal preferences in one's leadership thinking and behavior.

One's mental image or leadership paradigm comes about as a result of a combination of developmental experiences. It is through these developmental experiences that a conceptual leadership model is adopted and followed. The experiences that help to frame one's leadership paradigm may come from a variety of sources—from what one learns through reading, training, or education; or perhaps through personal observation of, or interaction with, an individual serving in a leadership position.[13]

The strength of one's leadership paradigm determines the extent to which one relies on it in acting out one's role as a leader. That strength is determined by how much the conceptual model cognitively makes sense to the developing leader. In other words, if the developing leader believes that the leadership paradigm is an effective concept to model, he or she will adopt the model in an adaptive manner, overcoming his/her personal preferences. For example, a developing leader who has a personal preference for bottom-line results tends to be practical, logical, and analytical. This orientation does not favor team development. However, if the developing leader observes the positive effects of teamwork and cooperation as part of another's leadership paradigm, the developing leader can overcome his/her natural resistance to team work, adapt, and integrate the practice of stressing teamwork into his/her leadership presence.[14]

The type of adaptation just described is essentially what one needs to exercise to implement the L^4 model. Adaptation is required because the L^4 model does not come naturally. This balanced L^4 model contains elements which appear to be in opposition to one another. For example, the L^4's two major dimensions of thinking, *reality* (now) versus *vision* (future), are in direct opposition to one another. The same can be said for deciding, that is, *personal* (feelings) versus *logical* (analytical). How does one adapt and apply a model of seemingly opposing values?

The L^4 model can be compared to the yin/yang symbol of the Chinese religion of Taoism. This symbol represents the Taoist postulate which is the relativity of all values and as its correlate, the identity of opposites. The polarity of the traditional Chinese yin/yang symbol sums up all of life's basic oppositions; day and night, life and death, male and female, and the rest. One (time) yin, one (time) yang. Yin and yang are the complementary, interdependent principles, or phases alternately in space and time. They are emblems evoking the harmonious interspace of all pairs of opposites in the universe. The terms in each pair are not flatly opposed, for they complement each other. Each invades the other's hemisphere and takes up its abode in the deepest recesses of its domain; and in the end, both are resolved by the circumference that envelops them, the Tao in its eternal wholeness.[15]

True to this symbol, Taoism eschews sharp dichotomies. All values and concepts are relative to the mind that entertains them. The same can be said of the L^4 model. The values of the elements within the model should not be viewed as opposed to one another, but should be seen as complementing one another within the boundaries of the organization. So for the culture of the organization to become balanced, the opposing elements should be evoked by leadership as the harmonious interplay of these opposites complementing and supporting one another.

ADAPTING TO THE L^4 STRATEGY

Developing an L^4 strategy requires one to cognitively become aware of one's personal preferences, to understand the natural tendency to favor an unbalanced culture according to those preferences, and to consciously look beyond personal preferences to the formation of a balanced leadership paradigm. Awareness is the first major step in moving toward an L^4

strategy. As the term "strategy" implies, this is a means, not an end. It is a journey, not a destination. It is a continuous process of self-examination, reflection, and adaptation. It requires thought and action within the context of the L^4 model. It requires one to consciously review thoughts and actions on a continuous basis until it becomes routine to think in terms of the L^4 model.[16] It requires one to review one's leadership actions based on considering the development of a perspective for

- *cooperation,*

- *inspiration,*

- *achievement,* and

- *consistency.*

This is not an "either/or" proposition. It requires the cognitive effort of reasonableness in thinking and deciding in a balanced sense about the impact of one's actions as a leader. Essentially, the leader must strive to creatively balance opposites. At times it is difficult to maintain an awareness of all four cultural patterns and to see the value of all four. The need for decisive action on a timely basis requires leaders to choose a desired end state such as more team work, superior products, immediate results, or empowered employees. Once the goal is specified and pursued, it is difficult to value the elements of the opposite cultural patterns. The opposing pattern tends to be negated and ignored. The L^4 strategy leads to more comprehensive thinking, and it helps surface the value of positive elements which perhaps have been negated in the past. Pursuing the perfect culture (the L^4 strategy) leads to higher performance even though perfection can never be attained.

It begins with integrating the L^4 paradigm into the leader's presence.[17] The leader must adopt a mental image of the L^4 model as he/she thinks and acts. In other words, the processing of information and acting out of behavior must have as a reference a mental schematic, illustrated in Figure 5.3.

If the leader consistently thinks about and applies this model in leadership situations, followers begin to see a balanced pattern of leadership actions and behaviors emerge which tend to:

1. Foster teamwork, cooperation, harmony, and trust, while

2. Inspiring individuals by recognizing the importance of human needs, growth, and development, while

3. Advancing the organization to improve its performance, status, and reputation, while

4. Instituting the discipline to achieve consistent results efficiently and effectively.

Figure 5.3
L⁴ Mental Processing

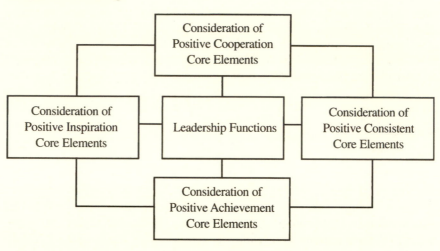

The implementation of this thinking approach can best be illustrated by applying it to a range of typical leadership functions. Figure 5.4 illustrates a partial range of functions and the respective L⁴ leadership practices which will help accomplish a balanced leadership approach. It is important to keep a number of things in mind when viewing the model presented in Figure 5.4. First, these leadership functions and practices are not, nor are they intended to be, prescriptive or comprehensive. Rather, they are presented as illustrations of how certain leadership functions can be carried out in a balanced way by adapting leadership practices which represent important elements in each of the four cultural patterns.

The second important part in using the model is to custom design it for the leadership position being considered. Every leadership position has its uniqueness in terms of the type of organization, level of responsibilities, and areas of accountabilities. I always ask leaders to begin by identifying those 10–15 leadership functions for which they are responsible. After they complete this task, I ask them to identify the accompanying leadership practices under each of the four cultural patterns that represents an integrated, balanced leadership approach.

Upon completing this, they have created their own leadership model— no one has done it for them. They will follow a leadership model of their own creation based on a balanced, integrated cultural model. They are adapting, not adopting. The problem I have found with other leadership models and approaches is they tend to suggest wholesale adoption of the strategies and practices presented. Following my approach, two leaders with similar responsibilities may come up with different practices for the

Figure 5.4
The L⁴ Strategy in Action

Leadership Functions	L⁴ Practices			
	Cooperation	Inspiration	Achievement	Consistent
Mission statement	Gain employee input in creation	Stress importance and worthiness of mission	Include challenging goals and objectives	Communicate clearly, concisely, and repeatedly
Productivity	Form work teams	Empower team members	Set stretch goals	Measure results
Quality	Share quality values	Stress importance of quality in helping customers	Set highest standards in industry	Establish procedures and monitoring systems
Safety	Seek ideas and suggestions	Show humane concern	Pursue superior safety performance	Enforce safety rules and policies
Customer satisfaction	Partner with customers	Demonstrate genuine concern and care	Help customers succeed!	Seek feedback from customers
Product/service development	Gain customer input	Understand and meet customer needs	Develop "best in class" product or service	Produce efficiently and effectively
Qualified work force	Promote team learning	Encourage personal development	Hire competent employees	Test employee candidates and periodically evaluate current employees
Community involvement	Help in community	Select worthy causes	Become model citizen in community	Monitor level of activities
Financial results	Share cost-cutting/revenue goals	Consider human impact of cost cutting	Set high cost-cutting/revenue goals	Establish budget controls and monitor progress
Satisfied employees	Create family/community environment	Adequately reward performance results	Set high performance goals	Hold individuals accountable
Motivated employees	Involve employees in work decisions	Assign employees meaningful work	Develop challenging jobs	Assess individual contributions

same function under each of the four core cultures. That is the beauty of the model. It is flexible in that it gives guidance to the development of leadership practices that are balanced, but does not dictate exactly what those practices should be. It leads, suggests, guides, but ultimately leaves it up to the leader to decide specific leadership practices to incorporate into his or her leadership presence. Once the leadership model has been developed and incorporated, it can be put into practice.

I have found this type of leadership change and development to be superior to those which focus on attempting to change one's leadership style. Trying to change one's leadership style is like trying to change one's personality. It is a well-accepted theory that personalities are pretty much fixed by the age of five or six. Slight alterations do occur as people grow and mature, but changes, if they do occur, are not significant. A more promising alternative is to change one's leadership presence, incorporating the L^4 strategy, enabling the leader to form an integrated, balanced culture.

6

The Importance of Setting Organizational Direction

There is an old familiar saying that states, "If you don't know where you are going, any road will get you there." That saying is applicable to the premise behind the L⁴ strategy. If you don't have an organizational leadership strategy, the kind of organization that evolves is left to the forces and factors impacting on it externally as well as internally. Even if you institute the L⁴ strategy and begin to move the organization toward integration and balance, will that move guarantee successful performance and growth? The answer is a definite "no," especially if you do not have solid organizational direction. Vision, mission, goals, and business strategy are factors that help determine organizational direction. This together with organizational effectiveness contributes to organizational success—superior performance and steady growth. I offer the following to illustrate the importance of organizational direction.

I was working with senior managers of a major division of a *Fortune* 500 manufacturing company who wanted to change the culture of their division. After several initial discussions with this group, they were convinced that the culture of their organization had to be reshaped if they were going to improve performance and become more competitive within their industry.

We began by analyzing where the division was and determining what changes had to occur within the culture to make it a more integrated and balanced culture. The top managers agreed that all key managers and staffers within the division needed to be involved in the transformational process. We designed and offered a leadership conference and offered several sessions to accommodate the over 200 who were invited to participate in the one-and-one-half-day program. The purpose of the conference was twofold. First, I presented a workshop on leadership, organizational culture, and performance. The purpose was to enlighten participants about the importance of all three in helping the division become more competitive. Through a series of lectures, exercises, and discussions, participants learned the definition and importance of organizational culture, how it is formed, how it is changed, how it can affect performance; and the value of an integrated and balanced culture.

Another part of the program was to break the participants into small discussion groups to brainstorm ways of reshaping the culture toward integration and balance. Each discussion group came back with some interesting ideas and approaches for reshaping the culture. Although ideas and approaches varied from group to group, one common concern that all groups expressed was this: "Reshape and balance the culture to do what?"

This was a shocking revelation to both me and the senior management group. We had assumed that all participants plus other employees knew the strategic business intent of the division. We were dead wrong. The corporate leaders had done a thorough job of articulating and communicating corporate vision, mission, and objectives. Because of this, we had assumed that those within the division knew and understood where we were trying to go. What we learned was that the corporate direction was too abstract for the division. It was too broad, too general, and not relevant to the operations at the division level. At that point, we had to stop and backtrack to reformulate organizational direction for the division. Once we did this, the culture reshaping process made sense to the participants and the exercises eventually resulted in changing the culture and improving the overall performance of the division.

THE ESSENCE OF LEADERSHIP

I relate this experience to illustrate the importance of understanding the true meaning of organizational leadership. What is the essence of leadership? This question was recently posed to four leading U.S. researchers and scholars who have been studying, teaching, and applying leadership theory and practice for decades. They were asked what can be concluded about the nature of leaders and leadership in organizations after centuries of human history and decades of psychological research. In other words, if four experts had to write a brief summary or synopsis of the state of the field of organizational leadership, for, say, the *Encyclopedia Britannica* or some similar outlet, what would they include?[1]

I was very interested in what each had to say about leadership. Each had an insightful, but a different perspective based on his background, experience, research, and personal biases. One of the findings the sponsoring editor of this exercise concluded about the four submissions came as no surprise to me; it is this: Basically, we have a definition problem with the term (leadership) that raises questions regarding measurement accuracy and consistency in research.[2]

I believe this widespread diverseness of opinion among leadership researchers creates the confusion among practicing managers about the true meaning of leadership. Adding to the confusion is the trend to distinguish between "managing" and "leading."[3] To eliminate this confusion, I combine the two. Here's why. There are various roles that leaders play (e.g., spokesman, coach, counselor, and teacher) and many activities in which they engage (communicating, planning, deciding, and motivating). Categorizing these roles and activities under "managing" or "leading" separates what should be coherently integrated functions that are required to perform two critical tasks. More to the point, leadership is a role that is entrusted to someone who has the responsibility to perform two very important tasks for the organization he/she is leading. So regardless of the title (i.e., supervisor, manager, director, administrator, vice president, or president), the two important tasks the leader must perform are:

1. *Establishing Organizational Direction.* Where is the organization headed? And how is it going to get there? It is the leader's responsibility to establish direction by determining vision, mission, business strategy, objectives, and goals. This requires a directional leadership strategy.

2. *Developing Organizational Effectiveness.* Once direction is determined, the strength, stamina, competencies, and agility of the organization must be developed by the leader. This enables the organization to serve its mission, achieve its objectives, meet its goals, and move in its intended direction. An organizational leadership strategy is required here.

These two tasks are interdependent. You can't effectively fulfill one and neglect the other. I point this out because in much of this book, so far, I have been emphasizing how to develop organizational effectiveness using the L[4] strategy. However, in emphasizing organizational effectiveness, I do not mean to diminish the importance of establishing organizational direction. If an organization has no sense of where it is going, organizational effectiveness becomes a moot point—an empty concept that is void of meaning and relevance to organizational members.[4]

In analyzing organizations who underperform, or worse, who fail, the source of their problems can usually be attributed to one or both conditions of a flawed directional leadership strategy and/or a weak organizational leadership strategy. Earlier in this book, I offered examples and illustrations of organizations that were underperforming primarily due to organizational effectiveness problems, which I described as unbalanced organizations. There are many organizations who underperform, and even fail, due to flaws and weaknesses in organizational direction as well as organization effectiveness.

The important factors that make up organizational direction are illustrated in Figure 6.1. When working with leaders, I ask them to assess the soundness of their directional leadership strategy by self-administering what I call the "3-C test." I ask them to critically review their organizational direction by posing the following three questions:

1. Is it *clear*?
2. Is it *concise*?
3. Is it *compelling*?

The first question has to do with clarity. Is the vision, mission, and business plan language clear and unambiguous? Does it plainly point out the direction of the firm so that everyone can easily understand it? And does it make sense and translate into meaningful words relating to the work roles and responsibilities for *all* members of the organization?

Next, is it concise? Is it brief enough so that people will remember it? Is it free from unnecessary and superfluous detail? I have read many vision and mission statements throughout my career, some good and some bad. One particular vision statement that caught my eye was of a company which was struggling and underperforming within its industry. To protect the identity of the company, I have slightly paraphrased its vision statement to read as follows:

Company Vision

Our company will lead the industry in satisfying customers with high-quality products and services. We are committed to accomplishing this through highly trained and informed employees who participate fully in the continuous process of improving performance, achieving the highest possible level of personal development.

Here is a case where a company attempts to incorporate too much into its vision statement by making it too broad and too general. The result is a vision that is not really clear and certainly not concise. I spent some time interviewing managers about the culture of this company and learned that no one could remember the content of this vision statement, although most knew one existed that had been written some years ago. This brings me to the next criterion for evaluating organizational direction: Is it compelling?

Compelling is a very powerful word. It has deep and far-reaching meaning. I like to use it as a criterion for evaluating organizational direction because it connotes an important and critical characteristic of organizational direction which is "to drive or urge forcefully." Is the organizational

Figure 6.1
Organizational Direction

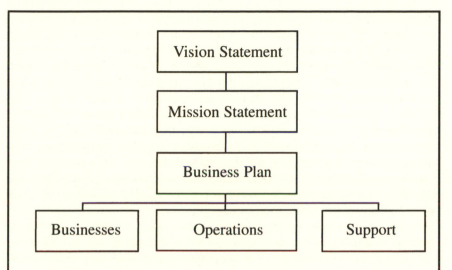

Establishing organization direction begins with a vision of where the organization is headed and goes on to point out how it plans to get there through the mission statement and business plan. This needs to be a coordinated, cohesive directional plan for all businesses, operations, and support groups.

1. A vision statement is the dream of the future or the ideal of what the organization desires to become long term.

2. The mission statement defines the organization, i.e., products, services, customers and what it hopes to accomplish in the short term.

3. The business plan outlines the critical objectives in achieving its mission and the strategy designed to achieve them.

The application of this model will vary according to the size of the organization, but it includes the essential elements for defining organization direction.

direction compelling? Does it provide the force to move the organization toward its intended direction? This force is made powerful by a number of factors. First, is it current? Is the direction something that is fresh and up-to-date or is it something that is dated and obsolete? For example, a vision statement written several years ago and placed on the company wall to gather dust can hardly be expected to be compelling. Next, what quality of thinking has gone into setting the direction? Quality thinking is required to frame the direction so that it is provocative. It needs to arouse, to stir, to evoke, to excite, and to stimulate. If it is not intended to be provocative, it certainly is not compelling. It must also be sound. It obviously cannot be something that is absurd, stupid, or ill conceived. It must be based on solid assumptions and good business judgement. It should, for example, involve long/short-range planning, creative thinking, and business modeling which includes elements such as forecasting, customer analysis, competitive analysis, and "what-if" scenario planning. And lastly, it should be measurable so that progress can be tracked. If not, it is not compelling. People are not driven to achieve it unless they sense that their efforts and energies have contributed to some level of accomplishment. Such progress must be measurable and perceptible.[5]

Business history is replete with examples of organizations which have underperformed due to weaknesses in both organizational direction and organizational effectiveness. For example, why is Pan Am, which dominated air travel 50 years ago, bankrupt and out of business today? Why didn't Howard Johnson's, which in 1965 had sales greater than those of McDonald's, Burger King, and Kentucky Fried Chicken put together, come to dominate the fast food business? And why does Apple Computer, which excelled in superior technology and product innovation, continue to struggle in the technology marketplace it should be dominating?

These are examples of weak leadership performance. Leaders of these companies failed to establish solid direction for their organization which was clear, concise, and compelling. In addition to weak direction, each had flaws in their culture. Pan Am failed to do anything about its weak *consistent* culture which prevented it from modifying its cost structure in light of changing economic conditions brought on by deregulation. The airline, in essence, allowed its competitors to fly by them. Howard Johnson lacked an *achievement* culture orientation to critically challenge its business paradigm in light of changing restaurant trends. Apple Computer's culture lacked a *cooperative* orientation. Its strong achievement culture stressed a proprietary, hardware-focused business approach which failed to meet key priorities of business customers who wanted open systems, minimum hardware costs, and the broadest range of business software. These are examples of how impaired organization direction and organizational imbalance combine to create a powerful negative force that is the major source of underperformance.[6]

OTHER EXAMPLES: GE VERSUS WESTINGHOUSE

Look at the difference between two industrial powerhouse organizations who were at one time fierce competitors: General Electric (GE) and Westinghouse Electric. From December 1, 1983 to December 1, 1997, GE's stock soared 931% to $74. And Westinghouse? It rose 120% to $30.62½, with three-fourths of the gain coming in its last 12 months—after it said it would abandon the industrial business. On December 1, 1997, Westinghouse Electric officially ceased to exist. The conglomerate that 30 years prior to its extinction was composed of 172 divisions narrowed down to three: nuclear energy, process control, and government operations. It recently sold the three remaining divisions.[7]

It is instructive to analyze the leadership differences between these two organizations to understand how this possibly could have happened. During the period between 1983 and 1997, GE has had one leader, CEO Jack Welch, while Westinghouse has had four CEOs including Douglas Danforth (1983–1987), John Maurous (1987–1990), Paul Lego (1990–1993), and Michael Jordan (1993–1997). (Note: Gary Clark served for a six-month period following Paul Lego.) These two giant companies mirrored one another in many ways except in their directional leadership and organizational leadership strategies.

Jack Welch's organization direction has, and continues to be clear, concise, and compelling. When he took over at GE in 1981, he inherited an incredibly diverse manufacturing organization that produced a range of products from light bulbs to jet engines, to locomotives to plastic resin. Welch's vision at that time was to become a market share leader. So at the beginning of his tenure he announced: "Be No. 1 or No. 2—or get out!" In a very clear and concise manner, Welch announced that GE would only invest in businesses that were leaders in their industries. Businesses that weren't first or second in their global markets were fixed, closed, or sold. GE divested $10 billion of marginal businesses and made $19 billion in acquisitions to strengthen world-class businesses that would lead GE into the 1990s. This direction has always been compelling throughout his tenure by its challenging tone and dynamic nature. That direction has evolved to the company's current emphasis which is the six-sigma quality program with its goal of virtually eliminating all defects by the year 2000.[8]

To accomplish the ambitious goals of his organizational direction, Welch made moves to balance the culture. Recognizing that GE was an unbalanced command-and-control organization, he instituted a number of measures to bring the organization into balance. He instilled in his people the "spirit and soul" of a small company. Self-confidence, simplicity, and speed were emphasized and rewarded. He introduced tools like work-out and CAP (Change Acceleration Process) to eliminate bureaucracy and tap

the ideas of those closest to the problem. These programs stressed cooperation, teamwork, participation, and employee empowerment in eliminating waste and inefficiencies, and improving productivity and quality.
These moves instilled elements emphasizing the *cooperation*, *inspiration*,
and *achievement* cultural patterns, adding more balance to the corporate
culture. Under Welch, GE spends upwards of $800 million a year on train-
ing and leadership development—about half of what it spends on research
and development. It is focused on moving the organization (all businesses)
toward Welch's vision and creating a balanced and adaptive culture capable of anticipating and coping with change.[9] Essentially, Jack Welch set
the direction of his organization first, then moved on to shape its culture.

The leadership at Westinghouse is quite a different story. The organizational direction at Westinghouse during the same years when Welch was
leading GE can best be described as a rudderless ship lost at sea. First
there was Danforth (1983–1987). He created a sort of short-term management culture. His emphasis was on quarterly results, and as such it was
management by the numbers. Instead of growing and expanding into new,
potentially high-growth businesses, Danforth spent more than $1 billion
buying back stock. Shares outstanding fell by almost 20% during his tenure. During his reign, Westinghouse would dump businesses with a combined $1.3 billion in annual sales. His biggest divestiture was a cable
operation which he sold to a consortium of competitors for almost $2
billion. Although Danforth justified the sale according to the numbers and
other factors, many of his contemporaries feel he betrayed the vision of
former CEO Robert Kirby, who saw cable and broadcasting among the
few units that showed promise for fast growth. Danforth saw otherwise
and abandoned these businesses.[10]

Next were the Maurous/Lego years (1987–1993). Danforth recommended Lego, who was then 57, as his successor to the board of directors.
Maurous, who was then close to 62 and retirement, signed his letter of
resignation but was talked into staying on as chairman for two years to
give Lego, named president, some needed seasoning. This move turned
out to be a costly leadership drain on the organization. Several key, talented executives who would not work for Maurous left the organization.[11]

Despite these departures, Maurous managed to deliver impressive looking financial results during his two-and-one-half-year tenure. Profits expanded to double-digit rates, sales of continuing businesses grew almost
as much, and return on equity hovered at 20%. In the summer of 1990,
Westinghouse stock hit a record high of $39.375. It would, however, never
be that high again as Westinghouse was about to go into a tailspin. The
financial services division, Westinghouse Credit, showed hints of trouble
in 1989 when it had a slight income dip. As it turned out, when Lego took
over as CEO and chairman, he was faced with loans and financial arrange-
ments that had gone bad to the tune of $3.8 billion. The enormity of the

problem was uncovered in 1990 when Westinghouse realized that it would have to repay all debts and cover all loans of the financial services subsidiary unit. Lego was finally forced out in 1993 and replaced by Michael Jordan, an outsider, who came in and transformed Westinghouse Electric to CBS on December 1, 1997.[12]

The extinction of Westinghouse cannot be attributed to any one event or to any one leader. Rather, it was a series of events and a lack of a clear, concise, and compelling direction (four leaders with an average of only 3.5 years to show results) that contributed to the deconstruction of Westinghouse and its morphosis into a broadcasting organization. Adding to this directional weakness was a missing integrated and balanced culture formation similar to what was initiated and formed at GE under the leadership of Jack Welch. Westinghouse's organizational culture was as vague and ill defined as its direction. What seems to stand out the most about its culture was its devotion to the numbers and its emphasis on short-term quarterly results, which reflects elements of the *achievement* cultural pattern. Unfortunately, this short-term thinking did not give the organization the adaptiveness, vitality, and strength to overcome the severe hardships it faced during some very turbulent and difficult times.[13]

K-MART VERSUS WAL-MART

A similar comparison can be made between K-Mart and Wal-Mart—two very similar retail organizations with very different leadership approaches. These contrasting leadership approaches and their differing results are best demonstrated by analyzing the performance of both companies between 1987 and 1994.

Leading K-Mart was Joseph Antonini and leading Wal-Mart was the late Sam Walton, its founder. (Mr. Walton died on April 5, 1992.) Both organizations started in 1962, but K-Mart took a very different path to growth than did Wal-Mart. According to many Wall Street analysts, it was the leadership of the two organizations that contributed to their different fates.[14]

At the time Antonini took over K-Mart in 1987, he faced some major problems—old stores, broken-down fixtures, and other building structural problems. Also, his predecessors had neglected to implement computer systems which rival Wal-Mart was using to track and replenish its merchandise swiftly and efficiently. However, in spite of this, K-Mart was still way ahead of Wal-Mart. It had nearly twice as many discount stores, 2,223 to 1,198. And K-Mart had sales of $25.63 billion compared to $15.96 billion for Wal-Mart. Besides, Wal-Mart was still competing in the minor leagues with its stores sitting on pastures outside small towns. K-Mart, on the other hand, had stores on expensive urban real estate and competed against other big discounters.[15]

However, Antonini still viewed Wal-Mart as a competitive force. It was multiplying across the rural landscape of the United States and about to invade urban America and confront K-Mart. Antonini responded by devising a strategy of marketing and merchandising, which was his personal strength. He invested heavily in national television campaigns, hiring glamourous movie stars as K-Mart spokespersons. His objective was to improve the K-Mart image and cultivate store loyalty.

Sam Walton did not counter in kind, even though most Americans had never seen a Wal-Mart advertisement or a Wal-Mart store as late as the 1980s. Rather, he became obsessed with operations. Walton invested tens of millions of dollars in a company-wide computer system linking cash registers to headquarters, enabling him to quickly restock goods selling off the shelves. He also invested heavily in trucks and distribution centers, around which he located his stores. Besides enhancing his control, these moves sharply reduced costs which related to reduced pricing, which he believed would be a key competitive advantage.[16]

Walton was right. In three years, after Antonini took charge of K-Mart, Wal-Mart surpassed it. For the retail year that ended in January 1991, Wal-Mart had sales of $32.6 billion compared to K-Mart's $29.7 billion. And the amazing thing about this comparison is that Wal-Mart had fewer stores, 1,721 to K-Mart's 2,330. Although Antonini invested heavily in a frantic attempt to catch up, K-Mart was so behind that a November 1993 internal company report found that K-Mart employees lacked the training and skills to plan and control inventory. This led to major problems with warehouses being filled with merchandise at the height of the Christmas season, and cash registers ringing up wrong prices.[17]

The most telling statistic that contrasts the results of the two leadership approaches was in 1994. During the time period that Antonini was chairman, president, and CEO (1987–1994), K-Mart's market share had dropped to 22.7% from 34.5%. Wal-Mart's market share soared to 41.6% from 20.1%.

As it turned out, K-Mart's strategy was misdirected. In addition, and perhaps even more importantly, the real competitive advantage for Wal-Mart may have been its culture. Walton became a student of W. Edward Deming, who taught so much to the Japanese about improving their productivity and competitiveness. Walton even visited Japan with his wife in the 1970s, where he got his ideas on improving teamwork (*cooperative* culture) and empowering people to have more authority (*inspiration* culture). Although he believed in and practiced empowerment, he always was working toward achieving balance between autonomy (*inspiration* culture) and control (*consistent* culture). He also listened to his people and encouraged ideas. He introduced programs and contests to solicit ideas from employees. According to his own estimates, he figured to be saving $8 million a year from these ideas. Another practice Wal-Mart is well-known for is that its executives spent much of their week visiting stores, soliciting proposals from workers, and spreading the vision of reaching $100 billion in sales by the year 2000 (*achievement* culture).[18]

In Troy, Michigan, by contrast, was Joseph Antonini who thought there was not much to learn by visiting stores. After all, he had been a K-Mart employee since 1964, when he started out as an assistant manager. He had come to be known as a "Teflon boss" because ideas and suggestions for change slid right off. He did little hiring of managers from outside the organization because they might challenge him, and he disregarded or dismissed consultants who recommended everything from management/ organizational changes to changing marketing strategies. Joseph Antonini was finally forced to resign in March 1995.[19]

In summarizing about the important relationship between the two major tasks of leadership (i.e., establishing organizational direction and developing organizational effectiveness), I like to make an analogy borrowing from the field of testing. We are all familiar with tests or exams we have taken throughout our academic and work careers in order to pass courses or to get job offers. These tests are only useful and meaningful if they possess two psychometric properties called "validity" and "reliability."[20]

Validity is the degree to which the test actually measures what it claims to measure. It provides a direct check on how well the test fulfills its function. The determination of validity usually requires independent, external criteria of whatever the test is designed to measure. For example, if a secretarial aptitude tests is to be used in selecting promising applicants for secretarial jobs, ultimate "on-the-job" success would be the criterion. If we hire secretaries who scored high on the test but turned out to be poor performers on the job, we would conclude that the test is not valid.

The second property is test reliability. This refers to consistency of scores obtained by the same person when retested with the identical test or with an equivalent form of the test. If a child receives an IQ of 110 on Monday and an IQ of 80 when retested on Friday, it is obvious that little or no confidence can be put in either score. If we find the same inconsistent results with a number of people who take the test, we conclude that the test is not reliable.

So, in determining the worthiness of a test, we review two psychometric properties, validity and reliability. A test is valid only if it is reliable. In other words, if you don't obtain consistent results by the same person taking the same test over and over, the test cannot possibly be valid. So essentially, in order for a test to be worthy and useful, it must have both validity and reliability. Having one property without the other makes the test useless.

Similarly, if an organization is to be successful (i.e., serve a useful purpose, perform well, and grow), it must have both a sound directional leadership strategy and, likewise, a solid organizational leadership strategy. If an intended direction is absent or inherently flawed, it is highly unlikely the organization will become successful. On the other hand, having sound organizational direction does not guarantee success. A strategy to pursue and attain organizational effectiveness must accompany the organizational direction if a company is to become successful. Assuming an organization has sound organizational direction, how does one initiate and achieve organizational effectiveness? In other words, how does one implement the L^4 strategy to achieve an integrated and balanced organizational culture? This is the topic of the next chapter.

7

The L⁴ Strategy and Organizational Change

In Chapter 5, I described what it takes to become an L⁴ leader. Although these leadership behaviors contribute to shaping a culture of balance and integration, they alone will not be enough to rebalance an unbalanced organization. The organization must be transformed in order for this to happen. In other words, commensurate interventions and changes in structures and processes must accompany consistent L⁴ leadership behavior in order to institute substantive change in the formation of the integrated and balanced culture. What is required is the reframing and realignment of individual and collective beliefs to coincide with the thinking behind the L⁴ cultural formation.

The challenge in any type of organizational change is to overcome resistance to change from the members of the organization. Organization members interpret major new management initiatives through their existing mental models.[1] Successful implementation of any fundamental change requires a new mind-set; therefore, helping organization members develop a new mind-set is critical in instilling fundamental changes in order to implement the L⁴ strategy. Many organizational change initiatives fail because leaders lack a basic understanding of how people change. Consequently, they design and/or sponsor change initiatives that don't follow, or worse, outright violate basic principles of human change.

There is a model of change that I have modified and adopted that has helped me understand my own self-change process and that has helped others to change. This fundamental change process includes five stages that individuals go through in order to change their attitudes, values, and behaviors. I have used this model to help individuals (executives and managers) as well as organizations (members) change and improve their performance. I have seen and read about many theories and models of change but none have evidenced the strong empirical underpinnings as the one described in the next section.

UNDERSTANDING HOW PEOPLE CHANGE

My change model is based on extensive research findings in the field of psychology.[2] The model reflects research done on individuals who overcame addictive behaviors (smoking, overeating, drinking) through self-initiated and professionally facilitated change. Although we are not dealing with addictive behaviors in attempting to induce organizational change, we are attempting to change deeply held beliefs of organization members who are as resistant to changing as a smoker is to giving up cigarettes or an overweight person is to changing lifestyle (diet and exercise).[3] The following is a description of the five stages of change people go through in overcoming an addiction, and an exploration of how each stage relates to organizational change.[4]

Stage One is called the *precontemplative* stage. People who are in this stage have no intention to change in the foreseeable future. Individuals in this stage are unaware of their problem. They fail to see a solution because they don't see a problem. Friends and family may be aware that a person has an eating addiction, but the precontemplative sees no problem. If badgered by friends and family, this person may demonstrate change as long as pressure is on. Once the pressure is off, however, this person often quickly returns to the eating addiction.

In applying Stage One to organizational change we find members who see no need to change the organization. They may see changes as incomprehensible actions of a top management group out of touch with day-to-day operations. This resistance to change arises in spite of the best intentions of those responsible for change. People will remain in this stage and resist change because of self-interests, misunderstanding, and inherent limited tolerance for change. Comments from precontemplators reflecting their feelings include, "What's wrong with the way we operate now? I don't see any problems," and "What's this? Another new program to make more work for us?" Resistance to recognizing the need for organizational change is the hallmark of precontemplatives.[5]

Stage Two is *contemplation*. People in this stage are aware that a problem exists and are seriously thinking about overcoming it but have not yet made a commitment to take action. It is in this stage that the person weighs the pros and cons of the problem and the solution to the problem. For example, smokers in this stage struggle with the pleasures they derive from smoking and the amount of effort, energy, and loss it takes to stop smoking. They suffer cognitive dissonance. They enjoy the act of smoking but also recognize that smoking can cause serious physical damage and possibly shorten normal life expectancy.

In an organizational setting, a person in this stage sees the need for change but is not totally committed to change. He/she is not ready to give up the known for the unknown. Individuals in this stage may be saying, "I know we need to change our organization, but I'm not sure how this will affect my job;" and "Yes, I am willing to change, but I need to see others change first."[6]

Stage Three is *preparation*. People at this stage of change are intending to take action soon. They may even have made some small behavioral changes already. For example, smokers may have reduced the number of cigarettes smoked to five per day or delayed their first cigarette of the day by 30 minutes longer than precontemplators or contemplators. Although they have made some reduction in their problem behaviors, people in this stage have not yet reached a behavioral goal for effective action such as abstinence from smoking. They are, however, intending to take such action in the near future.

Organization members in this stage of change may have already adopted some slight modifications to their behaviors that have been proposed by their organization. For example, if an organization is stressing a new approach to total customer satisfaction, an employee may have made some overtures of being more polite and responsive to customers than he/she has in the past. He/she may be intending to take action and fully participate in the company-sponsored customer satisfaction initiative in the near future.

Stage Four is *action*. It is in this stage that individuals modify their behaviors, experiences, or environment to overcome their problems. This stage requires considerable commitment of time and energy. Modifications of addictive behavior in this action stage tend to be most visible. However, sometimes people equate action with change. As a consequence, they overlook the requisite work that prepares changers for action and the important follow-up actions required to maintain the change. A person who quits smoking completely for one day to six months would be considered in the action stage.

In an organizational setting, the person may have completed a leadership training program and abstained from using ineffective leadership behaviors (authoritative behavior) for a certain time period, say, a week or two. The major challenge for that person is to continue the changed behavior indefinitely.[7]

Stage Five is *maintenance*. Maintenance is a continuation, not an absence, of change. For addictive behaviors, such as smoking cigarettes, the cessation of smoking extends from six months to an indeterminate period, past the initial action. For some behaviors, such as cessation of smoking, maintenance can be considered to last a lifetime. Being able to remain free of the addictive behavior and being able to consistently engage in a new, non-addictive behavior for more than six months is a sign that the person is in the maintenance stage.

If we apply this to an organization, consider a training program designed to change behaviors to make a safer environment. We would consider a member of the organization in the maintenance stage if he/she adopted the safety behaviors taught in the program and practiced these new learned behaviors for more than six months. Stabilizing this behavioral change and avoiding a relapse to old unsafe behaviors are the hallmarks of maintenance.

It is well-known that people taking action to modify addictions do not successfully maintain their gains on their first attempt. With smoking, for example, successful self-changes take an average of from three to four action attempts before they become long-term maintenances. In other words, people with addictive behaviors relapse so that the change process cannot be viewed as a linear pattern but rather as a spiral pattern of behavior change. In such a pattern, we see those who relapse recycle through the stages and learn from their mistakes, and try something different the next time around.

The same can be said of members involved in an organizational change effort. For example, in an organizational setting, members are trying to adapt to and accept new behaviors associated with teamwork and cooperation. On the first attempt by the organization, they may accept and apply the new behaviors of teamwork the first time the concept is introduced to the organization. However, after initial attempts members may relapse into self-interest and self-directed types of behavior. As teamwork behaviors are reapplied and reinforced by the organization, these individuals may well recycle to accept and apply the teamwork behaviors.[8]

IMPLICATIONS

Mental health professionals who help those with addictions design excellent action-oriented and self-help programs, but then they are disappointed when only a small percentage of addicted people register or when large numbers drop out of the program after registering. The problem is that most addicted people are *not* in the action stage. For example, a smoking cessation program is offered in the community and the registration sign-up is low or a large number of people drop out of the program. The program sponsors fail to recognize that most addicted smokers are in the precontemplation or contemplation stages of change and not yet ready for stage four which is the action stage.[9]

This same type of stage mismatching explains why so many organizationally sponsored interventions fail to achieve their intended outcomes.

Companies sponsor major change programs (training and development) designed to help organization members to change attitudes, learn new behaviors, accept organizational values, and/or develop new skills. The design of these programs is usually action-oriented. However, the majority of organization members are not yet at the action stage of change. In other words, they are not yet ready for change. The lesson from this example is for organizations to design interventions that help members move from the precontemplation stage through the contemplation and preparation stages first before introducing an action-oriented intervention.

I once knew of an organization that purchased a company-wide program designed to improve relations between and among members of the organization. The program was based on the psychological theory of positive reinforcement. The premise of the program was to use "behavioral engineering" and rigorously condition individuals by rewards (positive reinforcement) to be cooperative and sociable. The company sent all its leaders (executives, managers, and supervisors) to an off-site training program that lasted for five days. Upon their return, they were expected to implement the techniques they learned during the five-day program. In addition to the training program, consultants were available to the organization to assist the leaders in implementing the program. The company spent close to a million dollars on a program that lasted for six months. The company disbanded the program for its lack of impact on changing the organization. Here is an example of a failed action-oriented program which was presented to people who were at the precontemplative stage.

In another case, I know of a company that was seriously underperforming to the extent that it was facing extinction. Management and workers of the company recognized the company had a problem and that something had to be done in order to save it. The top management team decided to bring in a consulting group that studied the organization and concluded that its managers were too soft and undisciplined. Workers were getting away with murder—coming in late, leaving early, taking long morning, lunch, and afternoon breaks, and just goofing off on their jobs. Productivity needed to be improved and the consultants concluded that the managers had to take on more responsibility to raise the level of productivity within the company.

The consulting firm sent in a team of consultants who went from department to department working with managers and supervisors on the job, showing them how to be "tough" and institute strict control procedures backed with an authoritarian command-and-control approach to leadership. The consulting group worked with the company for close to ten months. The company spent close to $2 million on consulting fees. Improvements were realized while the consultants were on site; however, gains of productivity were lost and receded to their former levels following the consultants' departure. Workers of the organization, including the managers, relapsed back from the contemplative stage to their precontemplative stage. It is unlikely that the firm will survive.

Organizational changes such as those described often fail because organizations that are eager to change and improve their performance want a quick and easy "fix" to improve the situation. They want to quickly "fix" the problem with an action-oriented program. They fail to realize how important it is to help members of the organization move through the first three stages of change (i.e., precontemplative, contemplative, and preparation) before moving into the action stage. Further, they fail to help members move from action to the maintenance stage. Borrowing again from the field of psychology, there are various effective techniques used to help individuals overcome addictive behaviors and whose principles can be applied to an organizational change situation. These techniques can best be described as self-awareness, support, and reinforcement, and are described in the next chapter.

8

The L⁴ Implementation Plan

The L⁴ Implementation Plan is based on the change model described previously and relies on the techniques of self-awareness, support, and reinforcement. The plan consists of two parts. One part is a major learning intervention consisting of lecture, case studies, discussion, and self-awareness.[1] The other part is reconstructing the organization's infrastructure (policies, process, structure, and systems) to coincide with the philosophy and thinking behind the L⁴ strategy.[2] Together these two parts provide a powerful force in helping organization members move through the various stages of the change process—from the precontemplative through the action stages and on to the maintenance stage. The L⁴ Implementation Plan is driven by a transitional team. This team usually consists of the top management executives of the organization.[3] They must understand and support the L⁴ strategy if it is to be effectively implemented throughout the organization.

PART I: THE LEARNING INTERVENTION

The learning intervention is designed to help members move from precontemplative through the action stages. Leaders are trained first to help them understand the meaning and relationships between leadership, culture, and performance. Sponsored and coordinated by the transitional team, the leaders (executives, managers, supervisors) meet in training sessions designed to help them:

- Understand the important role of leadership.
- Know and understand the direction of the firm.

- Understand the meaning of organizational culture and its impact on performance.
- Learn the importance of an integrated and balanced culture that is the basis of the L^4 strategy.
- Gain a self-awareness relative to individual leadership presence, preferences, and paradigms.
- Learn important elements of becoming an L^4 leader and custom design a leadership model for supporting practices.
- Assess where the organization is now, relative to the L^4 model.
- Discuss and recommend changes in the organization's infrastructure (policies, processes, structures, and systems) that will help form an integrated and balanced culture.

Follow the training of leaders, a similar but abbreviated program is designed and presented to members (employees) of the organization. Again, the overall purpose of the program is to help members move from the precontemplative stage to the action stage. Consequently, the program should be designed to do the following:

- Help members understand the direction of the firm.
- Help members understand the importance of an integrated and balanced culture of the L^4 organization.
- Engage members in a process of self-evaluation of the firm, where it is today and how it must change in order to become competitive, successful, and growth-oriented.
- Engage members in exploring personal changes to coincide with organizational changes.
- Help members understand the need to reconstruct the organization's infrastructure.
- Ask members for ideas and suggestions in order to achieve directional goals and establishing an effective organization.

In presenting this, I stress that direction for the firm must be well established before embarking upon the learning intervention. If organizational direction is not first established, participants of both leader and member sessions will be confused.

PART II: RECONSTRUCTING THE ORGANIZATION'S INFRASTRUCTURE

Members are always skeptical about intended actions announced by top management, so it is very important to demonstrate visible, substantive change to closely coincide with Part I, the intervention stage. As in Part

I, the transitional team leads and coordinates this effort. They are responsible for putting together a plan for reviewing and modifying the policies, processes, structure, and systems of the organization. They should solicit ideas and suggestions from others throughout the organization, but they should ultimately be the group which decides what gets changed, and how, in leading the culture formation toward integration and balance.

The training intervention is a great first step. It gives feedback to the transition team about the state of the organization relative to the L⁴ model. At this point it becomes pretty clear to the transition team about what cultural quadrants need special and immediate attention in balancing the organization. However, the first order of business for the transition team should be to review the existing organization's value statements for modification to reflect the L⁴ strategy. If value statements do not exist, then the team should write them.

VALUES

Value statements can be a powerful force in guiding the organization. By defining and promulgating shared values and beliefs, the foundation is created that supports the organization's reality.[4] Value statements, as currently written or unwritten, may be having a strong impact in the organization's level and direction of unbalance.

In working with a manufacturing organization's transition team, we confirmed after the learning intervention that our initial impressions were correct: the organization was unbalanced toward the *consistent* cultural pattern. This organization had no written value statements. What was guiding the behavior of the organization was a value system based on assumptions members had made over the years. These assumptions, described by members, are summarized as follows:

- Your job is secure, as long as you regularly show up for work on time and stay out of trouble.
- You stay out of trouble by strictly following the bosses' orders and established rules and procedures.
- Loyalty to your boss is paramount in maintaining job security.
- "Covering your butt" is very important to staying out of trouble.
- Getting along with others is important to your job security, especially with union people.

These and other similar assumptions strongly supported the contention that the organization was unbalanced toward *consistent* culture with some emphasis on *cooperation* and very little on *inspiration* and *achievement*. The transition team used this information in devising organizational value statements as the first step in reconstructing the organization's infrastructure.

A formalized statement of values should be drafted to legitimize value choices. These value statements should be used to express what is central to the organization's desire to establish an integrated and balanced culture. Companies who have sustained long-term high performance legitimize value choices and then live by these preferences.

The value statements should reflect the integration of elements of the four cultural patterns of cooperation, inspiration, achievement, and consistency. In some cases the value statements may be embedded in the organization's mission statement, credo, or vision. They may also appear separate and apart from the vision/mission statement. A good example of a company statement that reflects the integration and balance of the L^4 strategy is Merck & Co., Inc., which is a pharmaceutical company. Merck annually appears on published lists of "most admired," "best performers," and "best companies to work for."[5] Its company mission and values are shown in Figure 8.1.[6]

Merck's mission and value statement according to the L^4 model (i.e., cooperation, inspiration, achievement, and consistent) is an excellent example of a cultural foundation for integration and balance, as illustrated in the following examples.

Cooperation

• Merck emphasizes diversity, teamwork, mutual respect, and the importance of the family.

• It stresses Merck's responsibilities to employees and their families.

Inspiration

• Merck's mission is to preserve and improve human life.

• Merck strives to provide meaningful work and advancement opportunities to employees.

• It stresses Merck's responsibility to the environment and society with which it habitats and interacts.

Achievement

• Merck stresses *highest* standards of ethics and integrity.

• It attempts to provide society with *superior* products and services.

• It intends to invest in *leading-edge* research.

• It is dedicated to the *highest* level of scientific *excellence*.

Figure 8.1
Merck & Co., Inc.—Mission Statement

ABOUT US
http://www.merck.com

Merck & Co., Inc. is a leading research-driven pharmaceutical products and services company. Merck discovers, develops, manufactures and markets a broad range of innovative products to improve human and animal health. The Merck-Medco Managed Care Division manages pharmacy benefits for more than 40 million Americans, encouraging the appropriate use of medicines and providing disease management programs.

OUR MISSION

The mission of **Merck** is to provide society with superior products and services — innovations and solutions that improve the quality of life and satisfy customer needs — to provide employees with meaningful work and advancement opportunities and investors with a superior rate of return.

OUR VALUES

1. **Our business is preserving and improving human life.** All of our actions must be measured by our success in achieving this goal. We value above all our ability to serve everyone who can benefit from the appropriate use of our products and services, thereby providing lasting consumer satisfaction.

2. **We are committed to the highest standards of ethics and integrity.** We are responsible to our customers, to Merck employees and their families, to the environments we inhabit, and to the societies we serve worldwide. In discharging our responsibilities, we do not take professional or ethical shortcuts. Our interactions with all segments of society must reflect the high standards we profess.

3. **We are dedicated to the highest level of scientific excellence and commit our research to improving human and animal health and the quality of life.** We strive to identify the most critical needs of consumers and customers, we devote our resources to meeting those needs.

4. **We expect profits, but only from work that satisfies customer needs and benefits humanity.** Our ability to meet our responsibilities depends on maintaining a financial position that invites investment in leading-edge research and that makes possible effective delivery of research results.

5. **We recognize that the ability to excel — to most competitively meet society's and customers' needs — depends on the integrity, knowledge, imagination, skill, diversity and teamwork of employees, and we value these qualities most highly.** To this end, we strive to create an environment of mutual respect, encouragement and teamwork — a working environment that rewards commitment and performance and is responsive to the needs of employees and their families.

Source: Merck & Co. web site: http://www.merck.com. Reprinted with permission.

Consistent

- Merck does not take unethical professional shortcuts.
- It is dedicated to lasting consumer satisfaction.
- It strives to identify consumer and customer needs, and to devote resources to meeting those needs.
- It strives to effectively deliver research results.
- It seeks to maintain a financial position that delivers a profit.

Merck demonstrates how a high-performing company has drafted value choices that shape its culture toward integration and balance, which enables the organization to consistently perform at high levels, maintain adaptiveness, and pursue growth strategies.

REINFORCING MECHANISMS

Most people with whom I have worked in organizations are more action-oriented than they are reflective or philosophical. They tend to be rational, pragmatic people. If you can convince them of a need to organize and operate a certain way that will be beneficial to them and the organization, they will generally respond positively and move through the change process.

Assuming that members have gone through the stages of the change process using the learning intervention presented previously, they are now expecting to see and hear of changes and new ways of doing things in the organization that reflect the L^4 strategy, to help form a balanced and integrated culture. The value statement formation was the first step in conveying the organization's intent to shape an integrated and balanced culture. But value statements contain words, and words are meaningless unless accompanied by action. This action should include not only the behaviors of the leaders (executives, managers, supervisors) but other mechanisms to communicate and reinforce the stated values. These infrastructure mechanisms include organization design and structure, systems and procedures, and programs and processes. The following is a list of common, widely used mechanisms that help form the infrastructure and integrate the positive element(s) consistent with the cultural pattern it represents. The list is not inclusive but is intended to offer examples of different types of mechanisms listed under the cultural pattern the mechanism tends to emphasize and reinforce.

Cooperation Culture. Encourages people to work together, share, cooperate, and help one another achieve common goals.

Mechanisms

- Establish communication links to encourage cooperation and sharing.
- Create diversity in policies and programs.

- Devise team-based compensation.
- Designate teamwork and cooperation as a core competency.
- Offer "team" training and development programs.
- Create teams (work, project, cross-functional).
- Hire team-oriented people.
- Integrate staff functions with business units as partners.
- Provide leadership/facilitator training programs.
- Recognize and reward team accomplishments.
- Remove organizational barriers (e.g., rigid chain of command) to team work.
- Treat employees like family.
- Sponsor team-building activities (picnics, outings).
- Create learning teams.
- Remove formalities, pomp, and circumstance.
- Teach conflict resolution techniques.
- Make easy access of members to one another.
- Make team behavior part of performance appraisal.
- Publish organizational newsletter.

Inspiration Culture. People are inspired due to their shared beliefs with the organization about the importance of serving social needs and helping people grow and develop.

Mechanisms

- Empower people.
- Train and develop people.
- Support/sponsor community volunteer programs.
- Donate time, money, resources to charitable causes and organizations.
- Provide career counseling.
- Support family/work balance programs.
- Establish management open-door policy.
- Share profits with workers.
- Treat people with dignity and respect.
- Sponsor employee-assistance program.
- Establish ethical behavior policy.
- Treat all employees fairly.
- Provide day-care assistance.
- Recognize and reward charitable actions.
- Encourage membership and involvement in civic and charitable organizations.

- Make work meaningful and enjoyable.
- Hire and promote people regardless of age, sex, race, or religion.
- Provide adequate compensation and benefits to employees.
- Provide supportive management/supervision.
- Become an environmentally responsible organization.

Achievement Culture. Motivates people to perform at high levels and work toward being the best and achieving excellence.

Mechanisms

- Make quantum breakthroughs.
- Establish stretch goals.
- Encourage challenging the status quo.
- Push for radical innovation.
- Produce "best in class" products and services.
- Conduct long-term growth planning.
- Set goal to be number one or two in industry.
- Hire bright, achieving people.
- Implement competency-based compensation.
- Promote people based on merit.
- Strive to achieve world-class performance.
- Teach courses on innovation and creativity.
- Support research and development.
- Establish sense of urgency.
- Set high standards of excellence.
- Establish global strategy for market expansion.
- Push for continuous improvement.
- Recognize and reward achievement/excellence.
- Challenge conventional thinking.
- Encourage outrageous thinking.

Consistent Culture. Establishes rules, boundaries, and systems to help people achieve consistent results efficiently and effectively.

Mechanisms

- Establish structure that clearly assigns authority and responsibilities.
- Set clear objectives and targets.
- Establish management system documentation.
- Implement standard operating procedures.

- Establish standards, codes, and rules.
- Implement monitoring and measurement systems.
- Eliminate waste and inefficiency.
- Implement planning and budgeting.
- Establish good record keeping.
- Automate manual systems.
- Eliminate defects.
- Implement cost-reduction program.
- Eliminate unnecessary paperwork, tasks, and processes/services.
- Shorten product/service development cycle.
- Streamline business processes.
- Routinize necessary redundant tasks.
- Teach critical thinking and problem-solving skills.
- Establish auditing program.
- Institute inspection and testing programs.
- Monitor external variables (e.g., competition, customers, economy).

Which reinforcement mechanisms should be implemented and in what order is a decision to be made by the transition team. The learning intervention usually provides some excellent insight about the decisions relative to implementing reinforcement mechanisms. If, for example, participants of the learning intervention point out the culture is unbalanced toward the *consistent* culture with little or no elements of the other three cultural patterns, then mechanisms similar to those listed under the cultural patterns of *cooperation, inspiration,* and *achievement* should be immediate candidates for implementation. The important thought is to implement them in a balanced manner that reflects the balance of the organization's value statements within the context of the firm's direction.

In reviewing the implementation plan, it is important to note some major points which need to be emphasized if the plan is to be successful.

1. Leaders are key in changing and reshaping the culture. Their attitudes and actions must reflect the L⁴ leadership model presented in Chapter 5.
2. Culture change is not likely to occur unless it is done within the context of organizational direction. Members need to know where the organization is headed before they can seriously consider accepting changes in their culture.
3. The learning intervention must be designed to help members move to the action stage of the change process. This must include a strong and compelling case for changing and reshaping the culture. The argument must be strong enough to move members from the precontemplative through the preparation stage of change.

4. Changes in the organization's infrastructure must closely follow the learning intervention. These changes help move members through the action stage to the maintenance stage of the change process. These infrastructure changes are accomplished by using mechanisms outlined earlier in this chapter.

5. The L^4 strategy is a process similar to continuous quality improvement. It requires the leaders of the organization to continuously monitor the culture and search for evidence indicating its integration and balance.

9

The Making of an L⁴ Company

The implementation plan described in the previous chapter is designed for organizations that are at the organizational stage of mid-life or maturity. In recent start-ups or young companies, the approach is different—it is evolutionary rather than revolutionary. In other words, the early leaders usually provide the set of assumptions that forge or create the culture. Through persistence and patience, the leaders embed them in the mission, goals, structures, and working procedures of the organization.[1] This is an excellent stage of the organization's development in which to introduce the L⁴ strategy. I have worked with such a young organization since its early start-up days. The following is a description of a company that has successfully evolved following the L⁴ strategy.

Double G Coatings Company, L.P. (DGC), located in Jackson, Mississippi, began operations in May 1994 and is a joint venture between Bethlehem Steel Corporation and National Steel Corporation. DGC is a producer of hot-dipped galvanized and Gavalume sheet steels, much of which is destined for the light-metal building-construction industry. DGC has experienced great success. It already has exceeded its rated capacity and has developed a reputation for world-class quality and cost-effectiveness. It has been featured and honored for its early accomplishments by numerous industry/business groups including the following:

- Featured in *Quality Management*, "World-Class Operations: Taking Care of What Takes Care of You," June 25, 1997, published by the Bureau of Business Practices.[2]

- Selected in 1997 as Champion in Industry which was featured on MS/NBC.

- Nominated in 1997 as one of America's Best Start-up Companies.
- Received in 1996 the Mississippi State-Quality Award for Excellence.
- Received in 1996 the Super Achiever Award from Metro Jackson Chamber of Commerce.

I have been working with Sam Moore, president; Mike Meadows, plant manager; and the DGC staff since 1994. My role has been to help Sam and Mike create an integrated and balanced culture following the principles of the L⁴ strategy. I have served as consultant, trainer, counselor, and coach to this organization providing a variety of services in areas of strategic planning, management training and development, team development, problem solving/decision making, employee selection and development, and executive coaching. The effective leadership of Sam and Mike provide strong evidence of how leadership and culture formation can result in superior and consistent performance.

ORGANIZATIONAL DIRECTION

DGC is led by its president and senior executives who function in an atmosphere of consensus management to build a world-class steel coating company. This group of executives and other leaders have been selected based on their skills and values according to L⁴ elements and, further, are developed to apply practices using the L⁴ model. These leaders develop the strategy for the company with input and approval from its board of directors. DGC's strategic planning, actions, and performance evaluations are primarily focused internally at its four critical factors—safety, quality, productivity, and cost. The goal of the strategic development process is to position DGC as the unquestionably preeminent supplier of coated steel products to the light-metal building-construction industry and to maintain its leadership role. The basis of the strategic development process is the core value of continuous improvement of the critical factors. The process is never ending.

The DGC leadership team monitors the performance of the operation on a daily basis through a variety of internal reports and a flow of external feedback from its two parent companies and their end-use customers. This information is compiled, compared to the competition and various plan objectives, and analyzed by the staff and their departmental teams. General strategies to improve critical factor performance are developed. Then major elements are identified and specific action plans are developed by departmental and functional teams to address each strategy for critical factor improvement. Each plan is designed so that its impact is quantifiable and may be measured for effectiveness. Upon completion of each plan, the president and the staff prioritize its execution based upon the importance to the company and the resources that are available. The organizational direction of DGC is clear, it is concise, and it is compelling.

ORGANIZATIONAL EFFECTIVENESS

The elements of the L^4 model are evidenced through the company's culture and can be viewed through the cultural pattern lenses of *cooperation, inspiration, achievement*, and *consistency*. These qualities have been set in place by DGC's directional plan, which is shown in Figure 9.1.

The infrastructure of DGC has been designed to reinforce the organization's leadership strategy (L^4 strategy) of cultural integration and balance. Some of the primary mechanisms DGC uses to reinforce the L^4 strategy are as follows:

Cooperation Culture. Encourages people to work together, share, cooperate, and help one another achieve common goals.

DGC Mechanisms

- *Team Formation*: All employees are referred to as team members and each is a member of a particular work team. Supervisors are team coordinators, which reflects that supervisors are more facilitators, coaches, and advisors than they are "bosses." These teams meet regularly to analyze ways to improve the equipment and its operation.

  Cross-functional teams are formed to periodically review and update, if necessary, every standard operating procedure. These teams also resolve problems requiring multidiscipline input. They periodically review and update company policy and other issues, conduct planning and forecasting, and design and participate in training programs.

  Teams are regularly recognized and rewarded for accomplishments in productivity, cost, quality, and safety. Team members often proudly wear and display Double G hats, shirts, and jackets. Recognition also is done by company newsletter articles, letters of commendation, verbal acknowledgments, pizza parties, dinners, management cookouts, and other similar methods.

- *Compensation*: A variable compensation bonus is paid monthly to all team members based on the achievement of team goals. This is paid in addition to team members' base salary packages. Every team member from material handler to the president receives the same monthly bonus percentage based on the performance of the team.

- *Hiring*: Screening and testing procedures are designed to select new employees who fit well in a team environment.

- *Training*: Team members regularly participate in training sessions to develop team skills such as listening, problem solving, communicating, and team building. Team coordinators are also trained as facilitators for team meetings.

- *Fostering the Double G Family*: To foster cooperation and cohesiveness among team members, outside activities are regularly scheduled throughout the year for team members and their families.

Figure 9.1
Double G Coatings Company, L.P.—Mission Statement

Double G Coatings
Company, L.P.

─────────── **Vision Statement** ───────────

Double G Coatings is committed to positioning itself as the unquestionably preeminent supplier of coated steel products to the light metal building manufacturing industry.

─────────── **Mission Statement** ───────────

The mission of Double G Coatings is to provide a service that will satisfy the quality standards and needs of our customers at the most competitive cost.

─────────── **Philosophy Statement** ───────────

Develop and maintain a dedicated and participative workforce that will accomplish our mission. Involve employees at all levels in matters that relate to their needs, the needs of Double G and Double G's customers. Promote cooperation and teamwork. Recognize and respect the dignity of the individual.

─────────── **Critical Factors Essential to Success** ───────────

❖ Safety   ❖ Quality   ❖ Productivity   ❖ Cost

─────────── **Objectives** ───────────

❖ **Safety** - Maintain a safe, healthy and accident-free work place.

❖ **Quality** - Consistently produce the quality required by our customers.

❖ **Cost** - Continually improve operating efficiency and reduce costs to maintain a competitive position with the world-class producers on a long term basis.

❖ **Volume/Customer Service** - Maximize productivity while maintaining customer service and satisfaction and at the same time controlling costs.

❖ **Workforce** - Create an environment that will ensure an involved and highly motivated workforce.

❖ **Continuous Improvement** - Continuously improve all business and production processes.

❖ **Community** - Act as a good corporate citizen in the community.

An annual family day is conducted for team members and their families on company premises. Food and entertainment is provided for adults as well as children. Team members and their family members often present the entertainment (e.g., singing, dancing, instrumentals, etc.).

An annual Christmas party is conducted on company premises for team members and their families. Catered meals are offered and gifts are given to all children. Leftover gifts are donated to local charities.

The company acknowledges personal family member accomplishments in company newsletters.

Other outside activities are scheduled such as an annual fourth of July picnic at the local semiprofessional baseball game. Golf outings, bowling tournaments, and fishing tournaments are also held. All members are encouraged to participate regardless of their skill level.

- *Organizational Structure*: Double G is organizationally flat with only four layers from top to bottom. Member interaction between and with one another, regardless of job or level, is a common occurrence and is encouraged.

- *Job Sharing*: Team members have broad job descriptions and regularly help and assist other members outside their job specs who are in need of assistance. The attitude is to do what is in the best interests of the operation.

Inspiration Culture. Inspires people due to their strong beliefs in the organization's values of serving social needs and helping people grow and develop.

DGC Mechanisms

- *Serving Social Needs*: Double G is very active within the community where it resides. The company and the employees donate time, money, and resources to various causes, charitable organizations, and other non-profit institutions.

The company supports a variety of local and national charities, police, and fire departments, crime prevention, and DARE.

Team members speak at local schools about careers in technology and manufacturing. They also teach and support Junior Achievement.

The company sponsors tours of its facilities along with a presentation of technology in manufacturing to local schools and colleges.

Team members belong to and participate in a variety of civic organizations such as the chamber of commerce, manufacturer's association, and various local development councils.

Team members adopt a cause every year for Christmas, donating time, money, food, clothing, and toys to organizations who help those in need.

Team members periodically adopt a group (i.e., school or community organization) and donate time, money, and resources. For example, team members adopted a special-education school for mentally and physically disabled children and donated specialized learning devices and classroom furnishings.

Team members take up collections for special needs brought to their attention by fellow team members. For example, team members recently helped provide food and clothing to children from troubled or economically depressed homes.

State and local economic development councils frequently refer out-of-state companies that they are courting to DGC because they know DGC will give the state and the local area favorable and professional reviews.

• *Serving Team Members' Development Needs*: Double G supports the development needs of its team members by creating a work environment that supports personal growth and development.

The company offers a generous employee compensation and benefits program.

Initial training costs per individual exceeded the costs of a four-year degree at Mississippi State University. It still maintains an aggressive training budget.

The company cares for its members. When team members are in the hospital, they are visited by fellow team members. Flowers are sent to the sick and to funerals. Baby gifts are given to the newborn of team members.

The company provides special assistance to team members who are facing serious problems affecting their families.

Bargaining unit team members are motivated and encouraged to learn by a pay-for-knowledge system. The program encourages individual team members to learn and master as many job functions, within a line of progression, as possible. Once qualified in an advanced job function through practicing, written tests, and time on the job, the team member receives an increase in his/her base salary.

Non-bargaining unit team members are given periodic performance appraisals.

Team members are empowered to review and recommend any changes in their jobs, equipment, and methods which will result in improved operations. Equally, they are empowered to make decisions on performing their day-to-day job functions.

Employee surveys are administered periodically to gain team members' perceptions of the company's policies, practices, and working conditions. Results are shared with all team members who are invited to serve on a cross-functional team to resolve or correct perceived problems.

Team members truly care about serving their customers and their two-parent companies. They receive feedback on their performance reflective to quality, product, and service.

Achievement Culture. Motivates people to perform at high levels and work toward being the best and achieving excellence.

DGC Mechanisms

• *Striving for Excellence*: Double G is relentless in its pursuit of excellence. It maintains its focus through the following:

The company teaches and preaches total quality. It teaches members that total quality is attitudinal and makes no compromises in safety, personal and business ethics, the quality of its product and services, and productivity.

It recruits and hires individuals who have the competencies and the desire to grow, develop, and achieve.

The company is committed to continuous improvement and has teams that work on inexpensive and innovative ways to improve methods, equipment, and operations.

The company has installed state-of-the-art equipment and technology that is cost-effective.

It establishes stretch goals for its critical objectives of safety, quality, productivity, and cost.

Despite its early successes, the company neither views itself as "having arrived," nor ever will.

While the company's reward system is designed to reinforce team work, it also recognizes individual initiative.

- *Being the Best*: The company will not settle for second best. It is dedicated to being the best in its industry.

The company consistently communicates its vision to team members of being the preeminent supplier of coated steel to the light-metal building-construction industry.

It consistently strives to achieve a cost-competitive position with world-class operations.

The company maintains a very competitive attitude with its principal competitors.

Consistent Culture. Establishes rules, boundaries, and systems to help people achieve consistent results efficiently and effectively.

DGC Mechanisms

- *Employee Performance*: DGC maintains rules and systems to ensure a consistently high level of team member performance.

The company employs an attendance system that applies to *all* team members and awards points for lateness and absenteeism. Accumulation of points can result in disciplinary action including termination. This is one of many policies outlined in the "Team Member Handbook" to assure adherence to high work-performance standards.

It administers the same testing procedures for all hires to ensure conformity and consistency in recruiting and selecting qualified team members.

Standardized training and certification ensures all team members the same standards for knowledge and skill acquisition.

- *Operating Performance*: To ensure consistently high levels of operating performance, DGC adheres to certain processes and procedures.

Standard operating procedures (SOP) exist for all major tasks and operations. The SOPs are periodically reviewed and modified. All revisions and new SOPs are published, reviewed with all team members, and placed in SOP books that are located at each workstation.

Operating processes are closely monitored employing statistical techniques, where appropriate, to ensure compliance with the SOP.

DGC regularly monitors and evaluates its compliance with all state and federal environmental, safety, and financial regulations.

DGC manufactures its products according to the American Society for Test and Material (ASTM) Iron and Steel Product Standards.

- *Equipment Performance*: The company has modified, reprogrammed, or replaced virtually every line component furnished in the original turnkey project to enhance quality and/or reduce cost.

- *Customer Performance*: The company utilizes distinct customer profiles, statistical process control, and internal quality system audits to maintain consistent performance. To serve its customers consistently, it employs real-time production and inventory-control systems, dedicated service representatives, and the latest EDI transmission systems.

The Double G Company is an amazing success story, considering that it started from scratch and has become an efficient, world-class operation in just a few years. When DGC started, it had only *three* employees who had ever seen a steel-galvanizing facility; and there was little heavy industry in the region from which to draw people familiar with related processes or technology. Today DGC has a highly proficient work team which effectively functions in an automated, computer-driven, highly technical environment. The success it has achieved is a result of the organizational direction and organizational effectiveness provided by the leadership of two individuals, Sam Moore and Mike Meadows, who constantly strive to achieve integration and balance in shaping DGC's culture and who are reluctant to personally take credit for what they consider to be a "team" effort.

10

Understanding Conflict Within and Between Organizations

Conflict occurs within and between organizations as it can occur within and between families. Conflict arises when groups of people (organizations) disagree, argue, and fight because of a variety of reasons such as competing goals, differing perspectives, and/or opposing values. Much of this conflict can be explained by applying the L^4 model.

CONFLICT WITHIN ORGANIZATIONS

In a medium-to-large organization, certain assumptions can be shared across all the units of an organization. If shared values do indeed cross internal boundary lines, we would say that a strong organizational culture exists.[1] If those shared values reflect the elements of a particular cultural pattern, say *consistent*, then we classify it as a strong, unbalanced consistent organization. In other words, most if not all the subunits are mirror images of the larger organization in that each has an unbalanced consistent culture operating. If most or all the subunits are balanced, we would classify it as a strong balanced, or an L^4 organization.

However, if there are few, if any, assumptions that are shared between and among the units, we would say that a weak, stratified organizational culture exists. This signifies that no one set of values is shared between and among the units.[2] It implies that the organizational units have differing cultural patterns operating within various units. Some may be balanced, some unbalanced; some may be unbalanced in the same direction while others may be unbalanced in different directions. By definition we cannot classify a weak, stratified organizational culture as either balanced or unbalanced because there is not a strong enough cultural pattern to warrant such a classification.

So essentially, we have three types of organizations. The first would be the *strong, balanced organization* which is the ideal and what leaders should strive to achieve (the L^4 strategy). Negative conflict is kept to a minimum in this organization because balanced organizational values have been integrated into the organization. The next would be a *strong, unbalanced organization* in which most, if not all, units share the values of an unbalanced cultural pattern like achievement. The third would be a *weak, stratified organization* that has multiple cultural patterns operating within its units. Negative conflict is more likely to occur in the latter two types of organizations (strong unbalanced and weak stratified) primarily because of the competing or conflicting values that exist between them. This is no problem if the organizations are independent, but it does become problematic if organizations depend upon one another.[3] In the two latter cases, differing or competing values can create conflict of varying degrees, depending upon the direction of the interacting, unbalanced subcultures.

For example, if an organization is an unbalanced cooperation subculture and has to interact with an unbalanced achievement subculture, moderate conflict is likely. The cooperation culture's team approach will attempt to develop a relationship of peace and harmony. The achievement culture will, however, view this approach with skepticism because of this culture's emphasis on individual accomplishment. Not so if two subcultures are unbalanced, say, in the direction of the cooperation cultural pattern. In the latter case, the two like-unbalanced subcultures will attempt to avoid conflict and strive for harmony. Various combinations of unbalanced subcultures explain why conflict exists within organizations, and why unbalanced organizations have conflict between one another.

As previously stated, in medium-to-large organizations we are likely to find units with their own cultures. These subcultures go through a culture formation of their own with their own leaders. These subcultures are represented by functional/occupational groups, geographically dispersed groups; product/market/technology groups; divisional groups, and various hierarchical-level groups. These subcultures are defined as follows:[4]

1. *Functional/Occupational Groups*: Derived from technical and occupational cultures of the function (e.g., research and development, sales and marketing, and engineering).

2. *Geographical Differentiation*: Comes about as a result of an organization's growth and separation into several geographic units.

3. *Differentiation by Product, Market, or Technology*: Groups that differentiate themselves in terms of the basic technology they employ, the products with which they identify, and/or the types of customers they deal with.

4. *Divisionalization*: As organizations grow and develop different markets, they often "divisionalize" most of the functions into the product or market units.

5. *Differentiation by Hierarchical Level*: Layers of management in the hierarchy to create "reasonable" levels of accountability or spans of control.

Take, for example, functional/occupational groups. The forces creating functional subcultures come from the technology and occupational culture of the function. The engineering department hires educated engineers, the finance department hires accountants, the sales department hires sales representatives, and so on.

Most everyone is familiar with the saying "opposites attract." This is used mostly in reference to two people who romantically find one another attractive. For example, a shy person is attracted to an outward-going person and vice versa. It is said that opposites attract for a number of reasons with one most-often-cited reason being that each person complements the other. The shy person enjoys being with the person who is the life of the party while the bold, sociable person enjoys the quite calm company of the shy person.

Such is not the case between interacting groups with the organization. That's because cultural opposites result in what the word infers—opposition. Opposite cultural patterns oppose or repel one another. Here is a hypothetical example: The engineering department is constantly at odds with the human resource department and vice versa. According to the engineering department, the human resource department is a group of bleeding-heart liberals. The engineers view human resources' endeavors as "soft stuff" that pushes too much the importance of caring about employees. The engineers' attitudes are that the company exists to design, manufacture, and sell products to make a profit. If employees don't like the company, they can go elsewhere to work. On the other hand, the human resource department views employees as the company's most valuable asset. They see the engineering department as a group of cold and uncaring people who view and treat employees with little or no compassion. The result of this opposing value can result in conflicts, arguments, and stress and tension between the two departments. This is presented as a simplified example of two unbalanced departments which create conflict within an organization. Factor in other departments (subcultures) with formed values, and it is not difficult to imagine why chronic conflict can exist throughout an organization.

Not all conflict within organizations is intense. Some unbalanced subcultures get along better than others. For example, two unbalanced cooperation subcultures will have less conflict than two unbalanced achievement subcultures. As the accompanying Figure 10.1 shows, two interacting, unbalanced cooperation organizations will likely have a low level of conflict because both will attempt to create peace and harmony

Figure 10.1
The Interaction of Unbalanced Subcultures

Unbalanced Subculture A	interacting with	Unbalanced Subculture B	Likely Level of Conflict	Comments
Cooperation		Cooperation	Low	Both organizations will attempt to create peace and harmony.
Cooperation		Inspiration	Low	Mutual humane concerns make these two very compatible.
Cooperation		Achievement	Moderate	Individuality of Achievement will moderately oppose team approach of Cooperation.
Cooperation		Consistent	Moderate	Consistent culture doesn't go for "soft and fuzzy" team concept.
Inspiration		Inspiration	Low	Both organizations will strive to help each other grow and develop.
Inspiration		Achievement	Moderate	Achievement can be too absorbed in its own ambitions for Inspiration.
Inspiration		Consistent	High	Free and spirited Inspiration does not like the controlling aspect of Consistent and vice versa.
Achievement		Achievement	High	Each will try to outdo the other to show superiority.
Achievement		Consistent	High	Power and politics of Consistent will clash with ambitious goals of Achievement.
Consistent		Consistent	High	Power and politics of both spell conflict.

between the two subcultures. Since unbalanced organizations tend to emphasize a cultural pattern to an extreme (in this case, cooperation), the key values of that culture will be emphasized to the exclusion of others. When two unbalanced cooperation cultures interact, the interaction and ongoing relationship goal will be to "get along," to help one another, and to strive toward unification and cohesiveness. On the other hand, the interaction and relationship of two unbalanced achievement cultures is quite different. The overemphasis of being the best, being superior, and being overly ambitious makes two achievement cultures clash with each other because each wants to be the best. In order to be the best, you have to be better than any other department/unit (subculture) within the organization. Each tries to outdo the other; so instead of working together in the best interest of the larger organization, each will do whatever is necessary to achieve superiority, even at the expense of the overall organization. Unbalanced achievement subcultures feel they are superior to the general organization and, consequently, look down upon the rest of the organization. It is as if they are saying to the entire organization, "Look, we are smart, and you are dumb. We are the elite of this organization. No other department/unit (subculture) can match us." It is easy to visualize how two unbalanced achievement subcultures would collide when interacting.

I once worked for an electric utility company as a director of employee education and development. I conducted management development programs for this company that owned and operated several electric-generating facilities, including a nuclear facility. The nuclear facility was staffed by very bright people and managed by nuclear engineers, many of whom were officers from the Navy Nuclear Power program. This particular facility was located away from company headquarters and operated essentially as a separate facility. After conducting a number of supervisory and management development programs, attending numerous management meetings, and personally visiting the nuclear facility, I recognized that this subculture was an unbalanced achievement organization. The other subcultures of the company consisted of a mix between unbalanced cooperative and unbalanced consistent cultural patterns.

The climate at the nuclear facility was very intense. There were constantly changing and challenging deadlines, goals, and objectives which had to be met. This facility, although quite young (several years old), had a very high efficiency rating when compared to other nuclear facilities. This meant that this nuclear-generation station was producing closer to its potential than most other U.S. nuclear facilities. There was a constant push to maintain and exceed these and other performance ratings. In addition, most who worked there had disdain for the rest of the company (those from other generating stations, operations, and administration). They viewed themselves as the elite group, as reported to me by many managers and employees from other parts of the company. They (nuclear) were always right, and everyone else didn't know any better. Company policies and procedures were for everyone except the nuclear folks. They had special needs and created their own policies. When they had to interact with other departments and you were there, you could feel the tenseness. In joint meetings with other departments, you felt as though you were in a pressure cooker that was gathering steam and pressure and ready to blow at any time.

The company tried to overcome this by having me conduct joint management-supervisory training sessions consisting of nuclear managers and managers from various departments throughout the company. It was believed that managers from these different departments might bond by training together. It was during these sessions that I sensed levels of stress within the nuclear management team that concerned me. I visited the person in charge of the nuclear group and expressed my concern. He reacted by bringing out his files and records documenting the superior performance of the plant, as if to say to me, "Look at this evidence. We are great! Who are you to question our management approach?"

About two months following the meeting, an accident occurred at the facility. It was the Three Mile Island nuclear accident, one of the worst in the industry's history. It made worldwide news and set the nuclear industry back years. The cause of the accident was said to be a combination of human error and mechanical failure.[5] To this day I often wonder how much, if any, the culture of that facility had to do with the accident. I know the stress level that can be created by an unbalanced achievement organization. I also know that stress experienced by an organization is similar to the stress experienced by a person. If a person's stress level becomes too high, it leads to distress which further leads to negative consequences. For a highly stressed person this could mean ulcers, high blood pressure, a heart attack, or some other physical, mental, or emotional condition. When someone is stressed out for long periods of time, we know something negative will happen; we just can't predict what it will be. The same can be said of an organization. When it reaches a high level of stress and becomes distressed for a long period of time, something negative will almost certainly happen, we just don't know what it will be. I continue to speculate the degree to which the achievement stress of the Three Mile Island subculture contributed to the accident there.

Figure 10.1 presents probable levels of conflict between unbalanced subcultures. But what happens within an organization that has both balanced and unbalanced subcultures? In other words, what happens when an L⁴ subculture interacts with an unbalanced subculture? The balanced organization, whether it be an entire organization or a subculture, is responsive and adaptive. It can adjust to varying events or circumstances. That does not mean the L⁴ subculture submits to any other subculture, nor does it mean that it attempts to dominate other subcultures. The L⁴ subculture invites related subcultures to join with it and do what is necessary in order to help the overall organization succeed. If that means offering constructive criticism to other unbalanced subcultures, then it will do it. If it means offering support and assistance to another unbalanced subculture, it will do it. The L⁴ subculture becomes known as the organization with no axes to grind, no hidden agendas, and no power motives. It is the role model for other subcultures within the organization, especially the unbalanced ones. In essence, it is the ideal corporate citizen. It will make sacrifices when necessary to do so. It stands up for what is right and just. It will help the weaker parts of the organization. It will never try to show up other sister subcultures or embarrass or humiliate them in any way.

The question often asked is, "How can balanced subcultures form and survive in an unbalanced organization?" The answer lies in the structure of the organization. Of the several types of subcultures mentioned earlier, it is most plausible within geographically dispersed groups and within divisional groups. These groups are most often managed with a "hands-off" approach, allowing the geographically dispersed and separated divisions to be managed separately and independently of the corporate headquarters. The leadership of these groups may successfully form and maintain balanced and integrated cultures. This is much more difficult for groups that are usually a more integrated part of the organization, such as functional/occupational groups; product/market/technology groups; and hierarchical-level groups. In addition, these latter groups are more strongly influenced by their shared interests, occupational focus, or similar social standings, which favor more unbalanced than balanced culture orientations. In the final analysis, however, it is the leaders of the subcultures who can make a significant impact in initiating actions to form an integrated and balanced culture, using an approach outlined in the L⁴ implementation plan. This obviously works better when the entire organization is involved; however, it should not deter subculture leaders from initiating action to form an integrated and balanced culture within their respective organizations.

CONFLICT BETWEEN ORGANIZATIONS

Conflict between organizations becomes especially important when two organizations are to be joined together through a merger or acquisition. In a merger both organizations are treated as equals and the two cultures attempt to blend together without necessarily treating one or the other as dominant. In an acquisition, the acquiring organization becomes the larger culture of the acquired organization, which is viewed as a subculture. In either case, blending the two cultures can be problematic.[6]

The challenge of successfully blending the cultures of two organizations has been well documented in the literature.[7] In fact, studies show that, at best, less than half of all mergers and acquisitions meet intended financial expectations.[8] In response to the many failed mergers because of culture clashes, it has been reported that companies interested in acquiring or merging with others are now conducting culture audits to determine compatibility between the two organizations before mergers or acquisitions are completed.[9]

Why don't these mergers work? Why is it so difficult to combine organizations that in many cases are in the same industry or profession and serving the same markets? The reasons for incompatibility lie in the separately formed cultures of the two organizations. Imagine an unbalanced achievement organization merging with another unbalanced achievement organization. A high level of conflict is inevitable, with each organization trying to gain a position of superiority over the other after the two organizations have been merged. The various possibilities and likely outcomes of mergers can be predicted using Figure 10.1. Although this figure represents interactions between subcultures, it can also be used in gauging the compatibility of two proposed merged organizations.

What is the solution? How can the incidence of failed organizational mergers be improved? One enlightening approach that seems to have merit is the concept of conducting a culture audit.[10] This involves inviting employees of the acquired company or both merged partners to participate in a series of focus group meetings or completing a questionnaire to assess current culture qualities and precombination expectations. The only problem I have with this approach is the timing. I don't believe that an organization ought to be analyzing its own culture at the time of a merger or acquisition. If it does, it may find out that its own culture is unbalanced, and that its future partner's culture is also unbalanced at the time both intend to marry.

When two people get married, if one or both are not psychologically and emotionally healthy, the stress associated with integrating two lives will certainly not help either person.[11] In fact, the problem each or both is experiencing will probably worsen because for two people to live together requires healthy well-being and adaptiveness. It is much better for two adaptive and emotionally stable people to marry; the odds are much greater for a successful marriage. The same can be said for organizational mergers. Two incompatible, unbalanced organizations marrying will certainly be problematic and chances of reconciling their differences are slim to none. It essentially requires rebalancing two organizations at a time when both are trying to adapt to one another. Rebalancing one organization is challenging enough; rebalancing and merging two organizations at the same time is next to impossible. That is one of the primary reasons why so many mergers and acquisitions fail to materialize. Take, for example, a strongly unbalanced consistent culture of an acquiring organization merging with a strongly unbalanced inspiration culture of an acquired organization. An extreme example would be the U.S. Army taking over the American Red Cross. Some would speculate, saying, "Hey, that's not a bad idea. The military will teach the Red Cross some organization and discipline that it needs"; or vice versa, "The army could use some lessons from the Red Cross about the care and welfare of its people." This sort of complementing of one another sounds great—one organization adding strength in areas of weakness within the other organization and vice versa. Such, however, is usually not the case. The strongly unbalanced, consistent culture-based organization will act as a dominant merger partner in the marriage. It will fail to see its own weaknesses and force the acquired organization to adopt the elements of its own unbalanced culture.

All of this leads to the logical conclusion that organizations should start the move toward balanced integration sooner rather than later. The L^4 strategy implementation plan presented in Chapter 8 will help the organization begin the move in that direction. To move in that direction requires the selection and development of people to serve in leadership roles. This is the topic of the next chapter.

11

Selecting and
Developing Leaders

In Chapter 6, I stated that those serving as leaders have the responsibility of performing the following two very important tasks:

1. *Establishing Organizational Direction*. Where is the organization headed? And how is it going to get there? It is the leader's responsibility to establish direction by determining vision, mission, business strategy, objectives, and goals.

2. *Developing Organizational Effectiveness*. Once direction is determined, the strength, stamina, competencies, and agility of the organization must be developed by the leader. This enables the organization to serve its mission, achieve its objectives, meet its goals, and move in its intended direction.

Performing both tasks successfully would be considered superior leadership performance. In selecting and developing leaders, it is obviously helpful to identify the personal traits, characteristics, knowledge, skills, and behaviors that contribute to superior leadership performance. Since there is much similarity and overlap between and among the definitions of these attributes, they are frequently referred to as performance "dimensions." For example, if we identify "creativity" as an important contributor to superior leadership performance, would we classify it as a trait, skill, or behavior? The common approach is to refer to it as a performance "dimension," and avoid the polemics of appropriately classifying such personal attributes according to trait/behavioral/skill categories.[1]

Once we identify a list of these dimensions and describe each, the list should be helpful in hiring or promoting the right person, and in developing current and potential leaders. This is important because some dimensions are more easily acquired than others. For example, "listening" is a dimension that can be easily learned while "conceptual ability" is more difficult to acquire through learning. It is this very fact that has fueled the age-old debate as to whether leaders are born or made.

ARE LEADERS BORN OR MADE?

This question has been debated for years. There are two sides to this controversial question and proponents on each side who feel strongly about their positions. There are those who believe that natural leaders are born leaders. Proponents of this theory believe that the great leaders throughout civilization are those who were born with the gift and talent for leading. They maintain that leadership is not something you can teach. You either have it or you don't.[2] Those on the opposing side of the argument strongly disagree. They maintain that leadership is not something that is mystical or magic and certainly not an inborn talent. They believe effective leadership consists of a set of behaviors that can be taught and, if applied, can result in superior performance.[3]

Those who believe in the "leaders are born" theory support their position by pointing out that there are many flawed and inept individuals serving in leadership positions in organizations. Their reasoning goes like this: "See, this is what happens when you don't select natural leaders. You get a lot of inept leaders because you are trying to fit round pegs into square holes. It won't work. You can't make a leader out of just anyone— it's a genetically inherited talent."

Those on the opposing side argue that individuals who are poor leaders have not been properly prepared. They dismiss the idea that you can't develop leaders. They point to situations which are common in most organizations whereby individuals are thrust into vacant leadership positions and are expected to act and behave as leaders without any formal training. Their argument is as follows: "How can anyone take on a leadership role without extensive training and education in leadership? You provide training for even the lowest level jobs in the organization, yet you appoint people to leadership positions, provide no training or support, and expect them to succeed in a role for which they are unprepared."

Actually, both sides have valid arguments. I present this information to support my belief that the performance dimensions associated with Leadership Task 1 (establishing organizational direction) are deeper and more complex than dimensions associated with Leadership Task 2 (developing organizational effectiveness). In other words, it is reasonable to expect that one can more easily acquire the dimensions of Leadership Task 2 through training than dimensions associated with Leadership Task 1. This becomes more apparent upon reviewing the list of dimensions which follows.

THREE SETS OF LEADERSHIP DIMENSIONS

I have identified three clusters of leadership dimensions that contribute to superior leadership performance. These dimensions are the result of my own personal research and professional experience during the past 20 years. They are not intended to represent an all-inclusive list. There are other performance dimensions that could easily be added to my list. I have attempted to include what I consider "key" performance dimensions. I have listed the dimensions according to my two major tasks of leadership plus an added category of what I term "Requisite Leadership Dimensions."

Requisite Leadership Dimensions are basic, fundamental personal attributes which are required for superior leadership performance. To use an analogy, a secretary cannot become an outstanding performer if he or she does not possess some basic dimensions such as technical skills (ability to type and file) and interpersonal skills (ability to effectively interact with others). Similarly, a leader will find it difficult to align followers if he or she is not honest and trustworthy. Followers will seldom align themselves with a leader they do not believe or trust.

1. *Requisite Leadership Dimensions*. These are attributes which are threshold requirements for superior leadership performance for managers and executives and which support the effectiveness of other dimensions in the two major leadership tasks.[4] They are as follows:

- *Honest*: Maintains high standards of integrity, resisting compromises on basic moral and ethical principles.
- *Competent*: Pursues and achieves high standards of performance in professional/technical field or organizational position.
- *Straightforward*: Presents self in genuine, self-revealing, and forthright manner.
- *Fair-Minded*: Values impartial treatment of others and is unprejudiced.
- *Adaptive*: The ability to adapt to and work effectively with a variety of situations, individuals, or groups.
- *Persuasive*: The ability to sell others on ideas, approaches, products, and/or strategies.
- *Self-Confident*: Belief in one's own capabilities to successfully deal with situations, people, or events.
- *Inspiring*: Ability to model behavior to draw out or bring forth the best in others.
- *Ambitious*: Driven to pursue and complete difficult tasks or achieve challenging goals.
- *Imaginative*: Ability to think abstractly and creatively in generating novel ideas and approaches.

- *Intelligent*: Mental ability to effectively perform numerical, verbal, and logical reasoning.
- *Determined*: Unrelenting in completing a task or pursuing a goal.
- *Forward-Looking*: Open to change and constantly assessing the need to change and adjust for the future.

2. *Directional Leadership Dimensions*. The dimensions of this cluster differ between executives and managers in two major areas: complexity and time orientation. In other words, the task of establishing direction at the executive level of the organization is much more complex than at the management level. Plus, the time frame for planning is long term (three to five years) at the executive level and short term (six to eighteen months) at the management level.[5]

Executives

- *Industry Knowledge*: Level of knowledge of the company's industry (i.e., markets, competition, products, and technologies).
- *Company Knowledge*: Level of broad and in-depth knowledge of the company (i.e., its customers, constituents, capabilities, history, and systems).
- *Vision*: Having a compelling image of the organization's future that will motivate and inspire its people.
- *Strategic Planning*: The ability to understand the dynamic complexities of the company's external environment and to establish a long-term business plan accordingly.

Managers

- *Content Knowledge*: Level of knowledge of the manager's area (e.g., business, function, professional/technical area).
- *Mission Setting*: The ability to define purpose, goals, and objectives for manager's area.
- *Short-Term Planning*: The ability to develop business processes and action steps to achieve mission.

3. *Organizational Leadership Dimensions*. The dimensions for this cluster are those required to establish an effective organization following the L^4 strategy. These dimensions are classified according to each of the four cultural patterns that help form an integrated and balanced culture. They apply to both executives and managers.[6]

Cooperation

- *Teamwork and Cooperation*: The ability to promote team work, cooperation, and harmony within and between work groups.

- *Interpersonal Relations*: The ability to establish and maintain positive social relations with others.
- *Team Development*: The ability to plan and implement processes and mechanisms that foster and support teamwork within the organization.
- *Team Leadership*: The ability to apply roles, functions, and behaviors required for team leadership.
- *Conflict Management*: The ability to mediate and effectively resolve conflicts and disagreements by using objective problem-solving techniques.

Inspiration

- *Listening Skills*: The ability to listen carefully and pick out important information in oral communications.
- *Sensitivity*: The extent to which one relies on empathy and sensitivity in consideration of others.
- *Sociability*: The ability to relate to others in a friendly, outgoing, congenial, and good-natured manner.
- *Nurturance*: The extent to which one is sympathetic, caring, and helpful to others.
- *Developing Others*: Coaching others, providing encouragement, recognition, and giving constructive feedback.

Achievement

- *Emphasizing Excellence*: Setting "stretch" goals and establishing high standards of performance expectations.
- *Initiative*: Constantly challenging the status quo and fostering an attitude of continuous improvement.
- *Risk Taking*: The willingness to take sound, calculated risks based on verifiable assumptions that the benefits outweigh the risks.
- *Creativity*: The ability to initiate original and innovative ideas, products, and approaches.
- *Achievement Orientation*: The ability to create an achieving environment that promotes energy and motivation to work hard, striving to be successful, attaining ambitious goals, and completing difficult tasks.

Consistent

- *Analytical Thinking*: Ability to use appropriate problem-solving techniques in analyzing and resolving problems in an effective manner.
- *Directiveness*: Ability to get others to comply to one's directives which express his/her intent.
- *Concern for Order*: Striving to reduce uncertainty in the organization by establishing clarity, orderliness, and discipline.
- *Self-Planning and Organizing*: The ability to plan and organize in an orderly, disciplined, and planful manner.

• *Group Planning and Organizing*: The ability to direct the planning, organization, and completion of group activities.

Figure 11.1 includes a summary list of all the performance dimensions which, I suggest, contribute to effective leadership. As mentioned earlier in this chapter, some dimensions are more easily developed than others. Cognitive intelligence or higher order mental processing is required more for Leadership Task 1 than for Leadership Task 2. For example, it takes advanced mental capabilities to conceptualize and visualize a company's markets in a dynamically and rapidly changing environment, devise a strategic plan providing direction, and develop a supporting business plan to achieve strategic objectives. This is a very complex mental exercise that requires the highest order of cognitive skill development. The combined conceptual/analytical thinking capabilities to perform this task are difficult to acquire through development. This contributes to the "leadership is born" side of the argument. On the other hand, some performance dimensions that relate to Leadership Task 2 are more easily acquired through development. Skills, knowledge, and behaviors associated with teamwork and cooperation can be learned through formal training and experience. This supports the "leadership can be learned" side of the argument.

PREPARING ORGANIZATIONAL LEADERS

The problem facing many organizations is the shortage of leaders who have the background and experience that matches up well to the leadership performance dimensions listed in Figure 11.1. The source of the problem relates to the education and training that most have received. The most likely candidates to be promoted to leadership within organizations are degreed professionals/technicians/specialists. They include accountants, engineers, marketing professionals, lawyers, architects, computer professionals, and business generalists. Their schools have prepared them well for their chosen professions but not for leadership positions. Many are well trained but poorly educated. They have spent most of their college-learning years taking a large number of specialized courses to satisfy graduation requirements for, say, business, and perhaps another set of specialized courses for a minor, say, computer science. The result is a well-trained specialist who may one day be offered the opportunity to serve in a leadership role because of superior job performance, and the promotion may result in turning a very good business analyst into a very mediocre leader. Throughout my career, I have had many supervisors, managers, and executives express to me that they were totally unprepared to take on a leadership position. Many had taken only a course or two in man-

Figure 11.1
Performance Dimensions of Effective Leadership

Requisite Leadership Dimensions

Honest	Adaptive	Ambitious
Competent	Persuasive	Imaginative
Straight-Forward	Self-Confident	Intelligent
Fair-Minded	Inspiring	Determined
		Forward-Looking

Leadership Task 1 Dimensions
Establishing Organizational Direction

Executives	Managers
Industry Knowledge	Content Knowledge
Company Knowledge	Mission Setting
Vision	Short-Term Planning
Strategic Planning	

Leadership Task 2 Dimensions
Developing Organizational Effectiveness Using the L^4 Strategy

Cooperation	Inspiration	Achievement	Consistent
Team Work & Cooperation	Listening Skill	Emphasizing Excellence	Analytical Thinking
Interpersonal Relations	Sensitivity	Initiative	Directiveness
Team Development	Sociability	Risk Taking	Concern for Order
Team Leadership	Nurturance	Creativity	Self-Planning and Organizing
Conflict Management	Developing Others	Achievement Orientation	Group Planning and Organizing

agement and human resources that fell far short of preparing them for a leadership position.

The diverse performance dimensions listed in Figure 11.1 do not match up well with a business major undergraduate who goes on to complete an MBA. The profile of a person matching up well with the dimensions in Figure 11.1 is a person who is an adaptable, balanced individual with a well-rounded education. This would be gained from liberal arts courses, which are referred to as general education requirements (core requirements) that all students, regardless of their majors and technical training, have to take. The problem is that these core requirements are less demanding now than ever before and are watered-down versions of their earlier offerings. These requirements tend to include a year of English, a one-semester course in natural science, one or two from the arts and humanities, social sciences, sometimes an elementary knowledge of a foreign language, and so on. These general education requirements are far from sufficient in preparing individuals for the performance requirements of leadership dimensions listed in Figure 11.1.

It has long been recognized that while a liberal arts education does not prepare students for any particular job or life, it does enable them to bring broad vision and deep understanding, not quick or simple solutions, to their own world and the world around them. As one liberal arts college states in its advertising literature, its aims for its students are to instill habits of:

- Exercising self-discipline
- Valuing hard work and high standards
- Deferring gratification
- Setting priorities
- Working effectively with other people
- Being flexible
- Having creativity
- Knowing how to argue effectively and to use evidence to support one's position
- Selecting a position
- Making a decision
- Differentiating what is false from what is true
- Finding out what you don't know and what you do know

These aims of a liberal education support the performance dimension of effective leadership set forth in Figure 11.1. Organizations who are seeking to hire individuals who will eventually serve in leadership positions should be searching for candidates who have a strong liberal arts background as part of their education.

LEARNING THROUGH EXPERIENCE

In addition to having a broad and diverse education, it is also helpful to have a diversity of experiences in preparing for a leadership position. In fact, many human resources professionals and leadership trainers I have worked with over the past 20 years believe that experience is the best teacher when it comes to leadership development. I agree with the basic principle that experience is effective in preparing one for leadership; however, I believe that these experiences should be planned rather than serendipitous and that certain experiences should be a part of the experiential repertoire.[7] I would advise any one preparing to become a leader to gain experience in a variety of areas such as the following:

- *Consulting*: Helping clients identify problems, search for alternative solutions, select the best course of action, and assist in implementation. (You learn to hone your problem-solving skills and your interpersonal skills.)

- *Non-Profit*: Serve on the board of or work for a non-profit organization that has some social mission. (You gain an appreciation of serving social needs.)

- *Project Management*: Serve on a team as a member, and as leader in working together and leading a project to meet budget goal and time deadlines. (You gain an appreciation of doing your best with the limited resources of time, manpower, and money.)

- *Turn-Around Situation*: Take over a situation which needs to be dramatically improved with limited resources and within a defined time line. (You learn to rally people around a cause that is important to them.)

- *Sales*: Gain any kind of experience that relates to customer interfacing (i.e., customer service, marketing, selling, etc.). (You learn to appreciate that without customers there is no need for a company.)

- *Product/Service Development*: Work with a group or lead a group which is responsible for creating new products or services. (You appreciate how creative, achievement-oriented people can help a company by developing new and better products and services.)

- *Production/Operations*: Work in the section of the company that manufactures the product or delivers the service. Gain experience in production-quality procedures. (You learn the importance of rules, standard operating procedures, and guidelines.)

This is not an all-inclusive list. Rather, it is presented to illustrate the diversity of experiences that helps one develop the performance dimensions listed earlier. Staying in one job family, on one track, over a number of years does not adequately prepare one for the leadership requirements outlined earlier.

HELPING CURRENT LEADERS

Personalized executive assessment and development programs are currently available through universities and consulting firms. Among businesses this type of program is often referred to as executive coaching. A typical program consists of three parts: (1) assessment, (2) developmental planning, and (3) follow-up coaching.

This type of program can be very helpful to managers and executives if it is based on assessing the participating executive according to each performance dimension listed in Figure 11.1. A comprehensive assessment program evaluating the candidate according to each of the performance dimensions can provide a list of strengths and areas for improvement for the participating executive. From this list developmental recommendations can be formulated and shared with the executive. This list of recommendations can then be formatted into a developmental plan for the executive. The plan typically includes a variety of experiences, readings, seminars, workshops, and on-the-job initiatives the executive plans to complete during the following six months. Coaching is then provided to help guide the executive through the developmental process.

I have been involved in many leadership development programs during the past 30 years, but none have proven to be as effective as this approach. I have had managers and executives who have completed such programs tell me it was the most richly rewarding and highly impactful program they have ever completed. It has helped many professionally as well as personally, especially in defining their roles as leaders. I highly recommend this type of one-on-one executive coaching to anyone who wants to improve his/her leadership effectiveness.

12

Summary and Conclusion

I have always been awed by the realization that leading, at whatever level within an organization, is truly a dynamic, complex, and challenging responsibility. Leadership requires a thoughtful analysis and resolution of problems and issues that are not simply black or white: most challenges leaders face are somewhere in between, mostly in the grey area. These challenges are usually messy, murky, ill-defined issues and problems that defy linear thinking and lock-step problem solving. The complex issues that leaders typically face are questions such as: Is the organization's direction correct? What does the future economy hold in store for us? Are we making the right assumptions? Does our business design match our assumptions? Do we have the right organizational structure? Are we hiring the right people? Are we paying them too much? Not enough? How about our benefits? And are we motivating our people to do their best? Do we have enough employee discipline? Too much? And on and on and on.

I am sure it comes as no surprise to the reader who has experience as a leader that there are no simple answers to those kinds of problems and issues. Anyone who purports to have quick fixes or easy answers is either a charlatan or grossly misinformed. I certainly do not presume to have solved all the problems and issues that leaders will face by writing this book. What I have attempted to do is offer a framework and some principles to help clarify and guide one's thinking in addressing important and complex leadership issues and challenges like the ones previously stated. To help the reader recap the main ideas and principles presented throughout the book, I offer the following summary.

THE ESSENCE OF LEADERSHIP

While management scholars continue to debate the issue of how to define and measure "leadership," there can be little disagreement about the two major tasks a leader faces, which are as follows:

1. *Establish Organizational Direction.* Where is the organization headed? And how is it going to get there? It is the leader's role to establish direction by determining vision, mission, business strategy, goals and objectives.

2. *Develop Organizational Effectiveness.* Once direction is determined, the strength, stamina, competencies, and agility of the organization must be developed by the leader. This enables the organization to fulfill its mission, achieve its objectives, meet its goals, and move in its intended direction.

Establishing role clarification is important for leaders to understand. Ambiguity about one's roles and responsibilities often ends in frustration and disappointment.

TASK 1: ESTABLISHING ORGANIZATIONAL DIRECTION

This requires a directional leadership strategy. Organizational members need to know the strategic intent of their organization. It is the leader's responsibility to ensure that strategic intent is in place and well understood by all members. This would include the vision, mission, goals and objectives, and business planning. Leaders can use the 3-C test in evaluating their directional leadership strategy.

1. *Clarity.* Is it clear enough for all members to understand?

2. *Concise.* Can anyone remember it? Or is it so complex that even its creators can't remember the important components of the plan.

3. *Compelling.* Is it a sound plan that can be achieved? Is it based on solid information, valid assumptions, and effective strategic planning practices?

TASK 2: DEVELOPING ORGANIZATIONAL EFFECTIVENESS

Once the direction is set, what will the leader do to enable the organization to achieve its strategic intent? This requires an organizational leadership strategy. In designing a strategy that will help establish an effective organization, it is instructive to review the research findings on organizational culture. The evidence strongly suggests that there is a link between leadership, organizational culture formation, and performance. In other words, if the leader forms the "right" culture, the organization will experience positive performance results. The culture a leader should be forming is one that is integrated and balanced. An organizational leadership strategy is offered that leaders can follow in forming an integrated and balanced culture. I refer to it as the L⁴ strategy.

THE L⁴ STRATEGY

The L⁴ strategy is an organizational leadership strategy designed to establish an integrated, balanced culture which strengthens the organization's performance and enables it to become adaptive so it can achieve superior performance, consistent results, and sustained growth. The strategy essentially draws upon the positive elements of four institutional groupings to form an integrated and balanced culture. These four institutional groupings include the family, social institutions, the scientific community, and the military/law enforcement establishments. The four respective cultural patterns that emerge from these groupings include the following:

1. *The Cooperation Culture.* The cooperation culture emphasizes teamwork, sharing, harmony, and cohesiveness.
2. *The Inspiration Culture.* The inspiration culture places importance on individuals—fostering the human spirit and uplifting humankind to a higher plane.
3. *The Achievement Culture.* The achievement culture stresses the importance of striving for excellence and being the best.
4. *The Consistent Culture.* The consistent culture values predictability and order. It strives to consistently perform regardless of external conditions.

The challenge of the L⁴ strategy is to integrate seemingly opposing elements of these four cultural patterns into a meaningful whole. The key is to balance what appears to be opposing forces. When this is done, the organization enables itself to become adaptive and responsive to meeting competitive challenges, improving performance, and achieving critical objectives.

There is a danger, however, of overemphasizing one cultural pattern at the expense of others. In other words, if the positive elements of one cultural pattern are emphasized to an extreme, the organization can become unbalanced. This causes an out-of-sync condition that negatively influences the performance of the organization.

Out-of-balance conditions can be moderate or severe. A moderate condition calls for a "rebalance" initiative. This is effectively accomplished by an evolutionary process involving organizational members. It requires the involvement of members in analyzing the current culture and suggesting changes in the organization's infrastructure. This enables the members to become intimately involved in the change process.

The leader of a severely out-of-balance organization does not have the luxury of time in correcting the condition. This condition requires a counterbalance initiative and usually calls for a severe, radical action or a set of actions designed to quickly counteract the existing unbalanced condition. In most cases, the leader unilaterally makes the decisions in counterbalancing the organization. Unfortunately, a counterbalance initiative is usually counter to the culture and is so radical that it causes a shock to the system.

The important lesson to be learned from unbalanced organizations is that leaders should take the initiative to create integrated, balanced cultures sooner rather than later. Although cultures may not be sending clear and urgent messages that they need reforming, the examples of out-of-balance organizations presented throughout this book should inspire leaders to be proactive rather than reactive in dealing with culture formation.

THE L⁴ LEADER

Establishing an effective organization using the L^4 strategy challenges one to explore his/her leadership presence. This is not the same as leadership style. Leadership presence is the living out of knowledge and values. It is an extension of a leader's way of being. Leadership style has more to do with things like voice, gesture, appearance, posture, emotional tone, and general manner. Leadership presence is a more powerful force in affecting culture than is leadership style.

One's leadership presence is reflected by two factors: one's thinking system and one's personal leadership paradigm. A person's thinking preference quite naturally leads one to favor a particular cultural pattern. That's because people are strongly influenced by the structure of their human consciousness. Carl Jung's theory can be applied in explaining how individual differences in thinking and deciding affect a leader's preference to favor a certain cultural pattern. In other words, leaders have a natural tendency to form an unbalanced culture.

That preference can be offset by one's personal leadership paradigm. For example, if one has a mental model of leadership that includes principles and practices that prove to be effective in running an organization, the leader can adopt the those principles and practices even though they may run counter to his/her thinking preferences. This adaptive thinking is what is required to become an L^4 leader. The L^4 strategy presents a mental model for the leader to use in developing a perspective for the four cultural patterns including cooperation, inspiration, achievement, and consistency. By integrating the L^4 paradigm into one's leadership presence, one can develop a leadership approach that considers the important positive elements of each of the four cultural patterns. This approach helps the leader form an integrated and balanced culture which successful organizations seem to have. Examples of L^4 organizations who have reputations as successful performers are presented throughout this book.

LEADERSHIP: TWO INTERDEPENDENT TASKS

It is stated throughout this book that a leader must develop a directional leadership strategy and an organizational leadership strategy. These two tasks are interdependent; effectively completing one and disregarding or ineffectively dealing with the other will result in an underperforming organization. In other words, a leader might have the greatest vision and accompanying business plan for the organization, but will never achieve the long-term goals due to a missing or flawed organizational leadership strategy. And conversely, a leader may work diligently to develop an effective organization using the L^4 strategy, but devises a flawed directional leadership strategy that moves the organization in the wrong direction. This principle can be used in studying and understanding why some organizations succeed while their counterparts underperform and/or fail.

The order in which these two interdependent tasks are approached is logical. Direction should be established before organizational effectiveness is developed. It is important for organization members to know and understand the directional intent of their organization first, and then to know and understand the L^4 strategy in developing an effective organization. Involving members and engaging them in a change process based on psychological principles of how people change is very important. Organizations that bypass critical stages of the natural human change process experience disappointing results.

The organizational change process in implementing the L^4 model is enhanced by reconstructing the organization's infrastructure (policies, processes, structure, and systems) to coincide with the philosophy and thinking behind the L^4 strategy. Changing and implementing programs, policies, and practices are needed to reinforce or support the integration of elements needed to balance the organization's culture. Examples of how new and existing companies perform this are presented in the later chapters of this book.

IMPLICATIONS OF THE L^4 MODEL

The L^4 strategy offers broad implications in leadership and organizational development. For example, it can be used to explain why conflict exists within and between organizations. Conflict occurs within organizations when various combinations of unbalanced subcultures interact with one another. The same can be said when two independent organizations with unbalanced cultures are joined through merger or acquisition. This resulting conflict offers partial explanation as to why only half of all mergers and acquisitions meet their financial expectations.

The L^4 model is also useful in selecting and developing leaders. It offers a framework for understanding the need for a liberal-based education for leaders of the future. It also offers a model that can be used in developing current leaders who want to improve their effectiveness and performance. The L^4 model has been useful in identifying important traits, characteristics, and behaviors that contribute to effective leadership.

Like any leadership theory or approach, the L^4 strategy is not the complete answer to effective leadership and/or superior organizational performance. It is offered as a tool for all leaders to use in evaluating their current leadership effectiveness and exploring ways of improving upon it as well as their organization's performance.

Notes

CHAPTER 1

1. The first scholarly work on organizational culture appeared in 1979. See A. Pettigrew, "On Studying Organizational Culture," *Administrative Science Quarterly* 24 (1979): 570–581.

2. The study of the link between leadership, organizational culture, and performance is well documented in this comparative research essay. See D. Denison, "What Is the Difference between Organizational Culture and Organizational Climate? A Native's Point of View on a Decade of Paradigm Wars," *Academy of Management Review* 21 (1996): 619–654.

3. Consultants' interests in corporate culture accelerated during the 1980s and is covered in D. Robey's *Designing Organizations* (Homewood, IL: Irwin, 1991), in the chapter "Organizational Culture," pp. 385–416.

4. During the mid-1980s the influence of the culture perspective in conducting research began to wane, leading culture researches to attempt to revise the effort. See P. Frost's symposium "Rekindling the Flame," symposium presented at the annual meeting of the Academy of Management, San Diego, CA, 1985. The current level of interest still does not come close to the high levels of interest that occurred during the late 1980s and early 1990s, as evidenced by a drop in research papers and scholarly publications on organizational culture.

CHAPTER 2

1. The historical development of culture is briefly covered in J. P. Kotter and J. L. Heskett, *Corporate Culture and Performance* (New York: The Free Press, 1992), p. 3.

2. See H. C. Triandis, "The Psychological Measurement of Culture Syndromes," *American Psychologist* 51, no. 4 (1996): 407–415.

3. See Kotter and Heskett, *Corporate Culture and Performance*, chapter 1.

4. Ibid., chapter 2.

5. For evidence showing a relationship between organizational culture and performance, see Kotter and Heskett, *Corporate Culture and Performance*; R. Calori and P. Sarnin, "Corporate Culture and Economic Performance," a French Study, *Organization Studies* 12 (1991): 49–74; G. Gordon and N. Ditomaso, "Predicting Corporate Performance from Organizational Culture," *Journal of Management Studies* 29 (1992): 783–798; and G. Hansen and B. Wernerfelt, "Determinants of Firm Performance: The Relative Importance of Economic and Organizational Factors," *Strategic Management Journal* 10 (1989): 399–411.

6. E. Schein of MIT states that leadership and culture are two sides of the same coin and supports this notion throughout his seminal book, *Organizational Culture and Leadership*, 2d ed. (San Francisco: Jossey-Bass, 1992).

7. See Schein, *Organizational Culture and Leadership*, chapter 4.

8. Ibid.

9. Although I did not refer to the term "culture," I wrote about clarity and commitment back in 1984. See S. D. Truskie, "The Driving Force of Successful Organizations," *Business Horizons* (May/June 1984): 43–48.

10. The importance of integrating the appropriate values and behaviors in a balanced manner is covered by Kotter and Heskett in *Corporate Culture and Performance*, pp. 141–151.

11. There is wide agreement that the definition of culture consists of shared "elements" that provide the standards for perceiving, believing, evaluating, communicating, and acting among those who share a language, a historic period, and a geographic location. See R. Schneider and R. A. Levine, *Culture Theory: Essays on Mind, Self, and Emotion* (Cambridge: Cambridge University Press, 1984). The term "elements" was applied by Schein to describe shared assumptions by members of groups or organizations. See Schein, *Organizational Culture and Leadership*, chapter 3.

12. See Schein, *Organizational Culture and Leadership*, chapter 3.

13. This is what Kotter and Heskett refer to as "healthy" and "unhealthy" cultures in *Corporate Culture and Performance*.

14. As W. A. Scott points out, most institutional scholars agree that organizations are deeply embedded in institutional contexts. A given organization is supported and constrained by institutional forces. Also, a given organization may incorporate institutional elements in the form of cultures, structures, or routines into its own system. See W. A. Scott, *Institutions and Organizations* (Thousand Oaks, CA: Sage Publications, 1995), p. 55.

15. Positive values are those which, according to management researchers, contribute to organizational effectiveness and superior, long-term performance.

16. Other writers have described models similar to the one presented here: "The Competing Values Model" was developed by R. E. Quinn in *Beyond Rational Management* (San Francisco: Jossey-Bass, 1988), pp. 44–65. See also F. Petrock, "Corporate Culture Enhances Profiles," *HR Magazine* (November 1990): 64–65.

17. Traditional cultures of Asia and Africa include many "collectivist" elements, while cultures of "individualism" are found in Western Europe and North America. Because of this dichotomy the word family by itself is not reflective of the elements contained in the *cooperation* culture. See H. C. Triandis, "The Psycho-

logical Measurement of Culture Syndromes," *American Psychologist* 51, no. 4 (1996): 408–412.

18. For an excellent treatment of the team development concept, see D. C. Kinlaw, *Developing Superior Work Teams* (Lexington, MA: Lexington Books, 1991).

19. Ibid.

20. This very much reflects the stewardship theory of management, which sees the individual as the self-actualizing man whose behavior is collective-serving. The theory espouses motivation through higher order needs (growth, achievement, and self-actualization). See J. H. Davis, F. D. Schoorman, and L. Donaldson, "Toward a Stewardship Theory of Management," *Academy of Management Review* 22 (1997): 20–47.

21. These kinds of values contribute to building a high-growth organization in which individual performance improves and heightens individual achievement drives of economic success. See C. Anderson, "Value-Based Management," *The Academy of Management Executive* 11 (November 1997): 25–41.

22. See Davis, Schoorman, and Donaldson, "Toward a Stewardship Theory of Management," 20–47.

23. For an expanded treatment on self-leadership see C. C. Manz, "Self-Leadership: Toward an Expanded Theory of Self-Influence Processes in Organizations," *Academy of Management Review* 11 (1997): 20–47.

24. This is termed "achievement orientation" and is defined as a concern for working well or for competing against a standard of excellence. This is considered to be very important for scientists. See L. M. Spencer and S. M. Spencer, *Competence at Work* (New York: John Wiley & Sons, 1993), chapter 4.

25. Ibid.

26. This culture is reflective of the Agency Management Theory (as opposed to the Stewardship Management Theory). Its model is the "economic" man whose behavior is primarily self-serving. He is motivated by economic needs (physiological, security, economic). See Davis, Schoorman, and Donaldson, "Toward a Stewardship Theory of Management."

27. The positive elements of the *consistent* culture are presented very clearly by R. Simons in "Control in an Age of Empowerment," *Harvard Business Review* (March/April 1995): 25–34.

28. In comparing management and leadership, J. P. Kotter, in *A Force for Change* (New York: The Free Press, 1990), labeled these behaviors and activities as management. He points out that planning and budgeting, organizing and staffing, and controlling and problem solving produce a degree of predictability and order that contribute to consistently producing key results by various stakeholders.

29. Ibid.

30. P. Koestenbaum, *Leadership: The Inner Side of Greatness* (San Francisco: Jossey-Bass, 1991) uses similar dimensions in describing the four strategies of leadership: vision, reality, ethics, and courage.

31. The application of the MBTI to other similar cultural models can be found in C. Fitzgerald, "Type Development and Leadership Development," in *Developing Leaders*, ed. C. Fitzgerald and L. K. Kirby (New York: Davies-Black, 1997), pp. 311–335. (Myers-Briggs Type Indicator and MBTI are registered trademarks of Consulting Psychologists Press, Inc.)

CHAPTER 3

1. This is essentially what Kotter and Heskett, in *Corporate Culture and Performance*, discovered in studying adaptive versus unadaptive corporate cultures.

2. This reflects a Gestalt approach developed by Laura and Fritz Perls. The word *Gestalt* translates best as "a meaningful whole" or "to complete." The Perls developed their philosophy from their observations that humans have a need to complete their experiences to make meaning of their existence. See F. S. Perls, R. F. Helferline, and P. Goodman, *Gestalt Therapy* (New York: Dell, 1951). The Gestalt model embraces the organization as a dynamic, integrated organism. As complex systems, the intellectual, emotional, physical, and spiritual aspects of individuals are constantly working toward balance. See "Person or Organization as a Whole," *Gestalt Institute of Cleveland, 1998–1999 Catalog*, p. 1.

3. *BusinessWeek* and the *Wall Street Journal* recently published a list of companies ranked by their financial performance during short-term (one-year) and long-term (ten-year) periods. For example, see "Shareholder Scoreboard," a special section of the *Wall Street Journal*, 26 February 1998, pp. R1–R20.

4. Compaq Computer, Intel, and Hewlett-Packard consistently appear as top financial performers in business and financial publications.

5. See Compaq Access, "Compaq's History." Accessed 1 April 1997. Available from http://www.compaq.com.

6. See G. Wheelwright, "The Near Fall and Rise of Compaq Computer," *TCP OnLine* 6, no. 1 (January 1997) [journal online]. Accessed 1 May 1998. Available from editorial@TCP.mindlink.bc.ca.

7. See Compaq Access, "Compaq's History."

8. See Intel Access, "Intel Mission and Values." Accessed 5 May 1998. Available from http://www.intel.com.

9. Ibid.

10. See D. Kirkpatrick, "Intel's Amazing Profit Machine," *Fortune* [online]. Accessed 3 September 1998. Available from http://www.pathfinder.com/fortune/1997/970217/tel.html.

11. See B. Schlender, "The New Man inside Intel," *Fortune* [online]. Accessed 3 September 1998. Available from http://www.pathfinder.com/fortune/digitalwatch/0511fil.html.

12. See Kotter and Heskett, *Corporate Culture and Performance*, pp. 58–67.

13. See Hewlett-Packard Access, "The HP Way." Accessed 2 June 1998. Available from http://www.hp.com/abouthp/hpway.htm.

14. See T. A. Stewart, "America's Most Admired Companies," *Fortune*, 2 March 1998, pp. 70–82.

15. See R. E. Stross and W. Woods, "What's a High-Class Company Like Hewlett-Packard Doing in a Lowbrow Business Like PC's?" *Fortune* [online]. Accessed 5 May 1998. Available from http://www.pathfinder.com/fortune/1997/970929/hew.html.

16. See Kotter and Heskett, *Corporate Culture and Performance*.

17. See D. J. Baxley, "IBM I/T Transformation Consortium Best Practices Benchmark," a report by IBM, Inc., 1996.

18. See J. Flint, "Company of the Year," *Forbes*, 13 January 1997, cover story.

19. D. A. Zatz, "Harnessing the Power of Change," *Ansom* (February 1994). Available from http://ssn.ssnlink.net/2zatzlodla/culture2.html.

20. See Flint, "Company of the Year."

21. See I. Sager, G. McWilliams, and A. Reinhardt, "IBM: Back to Double Digit Growth?" *BusinessWeek*, 1 June 1998, pp. 116–121.

22. See I. Sager, "How IBM Became a Growth Company Again," *Business-Week*, 9 December 1996, cover story.

CHAPTER 4

1. See "The Failure of Success: How Good Becomes Bad," in Quinn, *Beyond Rational Management*, pp. 66–78.

2. See F. Petrock, "Corporate Culture Enhances Profits."

3. See T. Y. Choi and O. C. Behling, "Top Managers and TQM Success: One More Look after All These Years," *The Academy of Management Executive* 11 (1997): 37–47.

4. See M. Brannigan, "Delta Air's Allen to Quit Three Posts," *Wall Street Journal*, 13 May 1997, pp. A3–A4.

5. See M. Brannigan and J. S. Lublin, "Delta Airlines Changes Style with New Chief," *Wall Street Journal*, 18 August 1997, pp. B1–B2.

6. Ibid.

7. See G. Herion and T. Rossi, "Ben & Jerry's Caring Capitalism," in *Hartwick Leadership Cases: Jesus and the Gospels* (Oneonta, NY: The Hartwick Management Institute, 1993), pp. 33–38.

8. Ibid.

9. See Geoffrey Smith, "Life Won't Be Just a Bowl of Cherry Garcia," *BusinessWeek*, 18 July 1994, in *BusinessWeek* Archives, pp. 1–2.

10. See P. C. Judge, "Is It Rainforest Crunch Time at Ben & Jerry's?" *BusinessWeek*, 15 July 1996, in *BusinessWeek* Archives, pp. 1–2.

11. See J. Pereira, "Ben & Jerry's Finds New CEO in Gun Industry," *Wall Street Journal*, 3 January 1997, p. B1.

12. See J. Pereira, "Ben & Jerry's to Post Earnings Rise of 39%, First Increase in Five Quarters," *Wall Street Journal*, 20 October 1997, p. B10.

13. See L. Lagnado, E. M. Rodriguez, and G. Jaffe, "How 'Out of the Loop' Was Dr. Frist during Columbia's Expansion?" *Wall Street Journal*, 4 September 1997, pp. A1, A6.

14. See A. Bianco and S. Anderson, "Is Columbia/HCA's CEO on the Hit List?" *BusinessWeek*, 4 August 1997, in *BusinessWeek* Archives, pp. 1–5.

15. Ibid.

16. Ibid.

17. In addition to other previous reference citings on Columbia/HCA, see G. Jaffe and A. Sharpe, "Inside Booming Columbia Home-Care Business," *Wall Street Journal*, 9 October 1997, pp. B1–B2.

18. See Lagnado, Rodriguez, and Jaffe, "How 'Out of the Loop' Was Dr. Frist during Columbia's Expansion?" pp. A1, A6.

19. See M. Schroeder, "Why Steel Is Still Bent Out of Shape," *BusinessWeek*, 1 July 1991, in *BusinessWeek* Archives, pp. 1–3.

CHAPTER 5

1. The notion of presence is taken from E. C. Nevis, *Organizational Consulting: A Gestalt Approach* (Cleveland: Gestalt Institute of Cleveland Press, 1987), pp. 69–87. Nevis' use of presence is used in a consulting model; however, it can be equally applied to a leadership model.

2. This definition is taken from Nevis' description of presence within the Gestalt framework. See *Organizational Consulting: A Gestalt Approach*, pp. 78, 79.

3. Ibid.

4. This finding is consistent with Quinn in *Beyond Rational Management*, who states that information-processing styles can be helpful in understanding why people have difficulty in seeing contradictory expectations that occur in organizations.

5. Leaders essentially enact their visions by constructing and/or modifying organizational cultures (i.e., by defining and promulgating shared values and beliefs that support the organizational reality they envision). See M. Sashkin and W. W. Burke, "Understanding and Assessing Organizational Leadership," in *Measures of Leadership*, ed. K. C. Clark and M. M. Clark (Greensboro, NC: Center for Creative Leadership, 1990), pp. 297–327.

6. See L. K. Kirby, "Introduction: Psychological Type and the Myers-Briggs Type Indicator," in *Developing Leaders*, ed. C. Fitzgerald and L. K. Kirby (Palo Alto, CA: Davies-Black, 1997), pp. 3–31.

7. Ibid.

8. See C. L. Walck, "Using the MBTI in Management and Leadership," in *Developing Leaders*, ed. C. Fitzgerald and L. K. Kirby (Palo Alto, CA: Davies-Black, 1997), pp. 63–114.

9. Ibid.

10. Ibid.

11. See L. K. Kirby, "Introduction: Psychological Type and the Myers-Briggs Type Indicator," pp. 10–11.

12. For a full description of the MBTI, see I. B. Myers, *Introduction to Type*, 5th ed. (Palo Alto, CA: Consulting Psychologists Press, 1993). (The Myers-Briggs Type Indicator and MBTI are registered trademarks of Consulting Psychologists Press, Inc.)

13. See Kotter, "The Origins of Leadership," in *A Force for Change*, pp. 103–126. He presents information on the development of leaders from childhood through adulthood.

14. See M. W. McCall, Jr., M. M. Lombardo, and A. M. Morrison, *The Lessons of Experience* (Lexington, MA: Lexington Books, 1988). This is an excellent treatise on how leaders learn, grow, and develop through jobs and assignments.

15. For an in-depth treatment on the Chinese religion of Taoism, see H. Smith, "Taoism," in *The Illustrated World's Religions* (San Francisco: Harper, 1994), pp. 123–144.

16. This is what Schein (*Organizational Culture and Leadership*, pp. 228–253) refers to as primary embedding mechanisms. He outlines how leaders influence organizational culture by a number of actions such as what they pay attention to, measure, and control; how they react to critical incidents and organizational crises; how they allocate resources; what they role model, teach, and coach; and the

criteria by which they recruit, select, promote, retire, and excommunicate organization members.

17. This approach is based on behavior modeling. It includes processes by which information (the L^4 strategy) guides the observer (leader) so that conduct (leadership performance) is narrowed from "random" trial and error toward an intended response (L^4 behavior). See T. L. Rosenthal and B. D. Steffek, "Modeling Methods," in *Helping People Change*, 4th ed., ed. F. H. Kanter and A. P. Goldstein (Boston: Allyn & Bacon, 1991), pp. 70–121.

CHAPTER 6

1. See A. H. Church, "From Both Sides Now: Leadership—So Close and Yet So Far," *The Industrial Organizational Psychologist* 35 (January 1998): 57–69. Church asked four leadership researchers and practitioners to answer the following question: "After centuries of human history and decades of psychological research, what have we concluded about the nature of leaders and leadership in organizations? In other words, if you had to write a brief summary or synopsis of the state of the field of organizational leadership, let's say for the *Encyclopedia Britannica* or some similar outlet, what would you include?" The respondents included Walter Tornow, W. Warner Burke, Robert Hogan, and Bruce Avolio.

2. Ibid.

3. Distinguishing differences between leadership and management was first explored by A. Zaleznik, "Managers and Leaders: Are They Different?" *Harvard Business Review* 55, no. 5 (November/December 1977): pp. 67–78. It was later pursued by J. M. Burns in *Leadership* (New York: Harper & Row, 1978) and most recently by J. P. Kotter in *A Force for Change*.

4. R. S. Kaplan and D. P. Norton talk about the importance of translating the vision, communicating the vision, business planning, and feedback in strategic planning. See "Using the Balanced Scoreboard as a Strategic Management System," *Harvard Business Review* (January/February 1996): 1–13.

5. For some excellent advice on establishing organizational direction that meets the "3-C test," read "Building Your Company's Vision" by J. C. Collins and J. I. Porras, in *Harvard Business Review* (September/October 1996): 65–77. Also refer to A. J. Slywotzky and D. J. Morrison, *The Profit Zone: How Strategic Business Design Will Lead You to Tomorrow's Profits* (New York: Random House, 1997). This is a helpful book on business strategy formulation.

6. See M. Hammer and S. A. Stanton, "The Power of Reflection," which points out that companies, particularly successful ones, get so caught up in carrying out their day-to-day work that they rarely, if ever, stop to think objectively about themselves or their businesses. In *Fortune*, 24 November 1997, pp. 291–296.

7. Much information on General Electric and Westinghouse Electric has been covered in popular business publications (newspapers and magazines). An excellent chronological analysis of Westinghouse from 1963 through 1997 is presented in S. Massey's series, "Who Killed Westinghouse?" *Pittsburgh Post-Gazette*, February 28–March 7, 1998.

8. See Stewart, "America's Most Admired Companies."

9. See Slywotzky and Morrison, *The Profit Zone*, pp. 73–90.

10. Massey, "Who Killed Westinghouse?"

11. Ibid.

12. Ibid.

13. W. R. King, a university professor in the Katz Graduate School of Business at the University of Pittsburgh, served as a consultant to Westinghouse from Bob Kirby's through Paul Lego's reign. He states that the most crucial of Westinghouse's problems were a lack of sustained visionary leadership and a lack of control systems. See W. R. King, "Westinghouse: What Went Wrong," *Pittsburgh Post-Gazette*, 15 March 1998, pp. C1, C4.

14. Background information on K-Mart and Wal-Mart are available through popular business publications. An especially insightful analysis on the comparison between the two was by C. Duff and B. Ortega, "How Wal-Mart Outdid a Once-Touted K-Mart in Discount Store Race," *Wall Street Journal*, 24 March 1995, pp. A1, A4.

15. Ibid.

16. Ibid.

17. Ibid.

18. For an informed, inside look at Sam Walton, see S. Walton with J. Huey, *Sam Walton: Made in America* (New York: Bantam Books, 1992).

19. See Duff and Ortega, "How Wal-Mart Outdid a Once-Touted K-Mart in Discount Store Race."

20. See A. Anastasi, *Psychological Testing* (New York: Macmillian, 1988), pp. 109–164.

CHAPTER 7

1. See R. K. Reger, J. V. Mullane, L. T. Gustafson, and S. M. DeMarie, "Creating Earthquakes to Change Organizational Mindsets," *Academy of Management Executive* 8 (November 1994): 31–41. This article focuses on overcoming the resistance that resides with the mind-sets of organizational members—managers and employees alike. They offer suggestions on how to avoid and, when necessary, overcome resistance to change.

2. The model of change was developed by J. O. Prochaska, C. C. DiClemente, and J. C. Norcross, "In Search of How People Change: Applications to Addictive Behaviors," *American Psychologist* 27, no. 9 (September 1992): 1102–1114. The model was a result of a 12-year program which was dedicated to solving the puzzle of how people intentionally change their behavior with and without psychotherapy.

3. Schein points out that what happens in culture change is essentially self-guided evolution through organizational therapy. Though leaders would not typically describe this as therapy, it is functionally the equivalent (for groups) of what individuals undergo when they seek therapeutic help. See Schein, *Organizational Culture and Leadership*, p. 307.

4. See Prochaska, DiClemente, and Norcross, "In Search of How People Change."

5. This is referred to as passive resistance which results from a failure to fully comprehend the change. See Reger et al., "Creating Earthquakes to Change Organizational Mindsets," pp. 34–35.

6. Ambiguity and uncertainty at Stage Two can result in active resistance resulting in cognitive opposition. See Reger et al., "Creating Earthquakes to Change Organizational Mindsets."

7. Reger et al. advise at this stage that change occurs when the gap between current and ideal is large enough to create the stress necessary for members to desire to change, but the dissimilarities are not so great that the ideal is perceived to be unattainable. See Reger et al., "Creating Earthquakes to Change Organizational Mindsets."

8. This is what Reger et al. recommend and term "tectonic" change, which is applying a series of mid-range actions to implementing fundamental changes. Initial successes encourage additional changes. See Reger et al., "Creating Earthquakes to Change Organizational Mindsets."

9. See "Mismatching Stage and Treatment" by Prochaska, DiClemente, and Norcross in "In Search of How People Change."

CHAPTER 8

1. This model of change, like many others, is derived from R. Beckard, *Organization Development: Strategies and Models* (Reading, MA: Addison-Wesley, 1969); R. Beckard and R. T. Harris, *Organizational Transitions: Managing Complex Change* (Reading, MA: Addison-Wesley, 1987); and R. Beckard and W. Pritchard, *Changing the Essence: The Art of Creating Fundamental Change in Organizations* (San Francisco: Jossey-Bass, 1992). These principles are as follows: (a) Why change? Determine the need for change and determine the degree of choice about whether to change; (b) Describe the desired future state; (c) Describe the present state; (d) Compare the "desired" and "present" states; (e) Determine how to get from here to there; and (f) Managing the transition state. See A. M. Freedman, "The Undiscussable Sides of Implementing Transformational Change," *Consulting Psychology Journal: Practice and Research* 49, no. 1 (Winter 1997): 51–76.

2. Earlier, I referred to Schein's primary embedding mechanisms in describing L^4 leadership actions. Restructuring relates to his concept of secondary articulation and reinforcement mechanisms in changing culture. They include organizational design and structure; organizational systems and procedures; and organizational rites and rituals, among others. See Schein, *Organizational Culture and Leadership*, pp. 228–254.

3. This transitional team is what J. Kotter refers to as "The Guiding Coalition." He suggests four key characteristics that the guiding coalition should have, including position power, expertise, credibility, and leadership. See J. Kotter, *Leading Change* (Boston: Harvard Business School Press, 1996), pp. 51–66.

4. J. Chatman and K. A. Jehn found in their study that specific cultural values were associated with levels of industry technology and growth. See J. Chatman and K. A. Jehn, "Assessing the Relationship between Industry Characteristics and Organizational Culture: How Different Can You Be?" *Academy of Management Journal* 37, no. 3 (June 1994): 522–553.

5. Merck appeared on many top lists of performers during 1998, including *Fortune*'s "America's Most Admired Companies," in which it was ranked tenth.

6. See Merck Access, "Merck & Co., Inc. Mission Statement." Accessed 7 July 1998. Available from http://www.merck.com.

CHAPTER 9

1. See Schein, "The Dynamics of Culture Change and Leadership in Young Organizations," in *Organizational Culture and Leadership*, pp. 297–312.

2. See "World-Class Operations: Taking Care of What Takes Care of You," *Quality Management*, Bureau of Business Practice Newsletter, 25 June 1997, pp. 1–4.

CHAPTER 10

1. Kotter and Heskett describe this "strong" culture as one in which most managers share a set of relatively consistent values and methods of doing business. New employees adopt these values very quickly. See Kotter and Heskett, *Corporate Culture and Performance*, pp. 15–27.

2. Ibid. Kotter and Heskett compare "strong" and weak cultures.

3. See D. Robey, "Differentiation, Interdependence, and Conflict," in *Designing Organizations*, pp. 151–179.

4. See Schein, *Organizational Culture and Leadership*, pp. 256–275. Schein also includes three other groups: (1) mergers and acquisitions; (2) joint ventures, strategic alliances, and multiorganizational units; and (3) structural opposition groups.

5. The cause of the Three Mile Island nuclear accident (a combination of human error and mechanical failure) is well documented and available in public records, including the archives of the Nuclear Regulatory Commission.

6. See Schein, "Mergers and Acquisitions," in *Organizational Culture and Leadership*, pp. 268–271.

7. See S. Cartwright and C. L. Cooper, "The Role of Compatibility in Successful Organizational Marriage," *Academy of Management Executive* 7, no. 2 (1993): 57–69. This is an excellent article based on research findings; it examines the role of culture compatibility in determining venture outcomes.

8. See S. Sleek, "Some Corporate Mergers, Like Marriages, End Up on the Rocks," *Monitor*, the American Psychological Association (July 1998): 13. Also see M. L. Marks and P. H. Mirvis, *Joining Forces: Making One Plus One Equal Three in Mergers, Acquisitions, and Alliances* (San Francisco: Jossey-Bass, 1998). Also see G. Mottola, S. Gaertner, and J. Dovidio, "How Groups Merge: The Effects of Merger Integration Patterns on Anticipated Commitment to the Merged Organization," *Journal of Applied Social Psychology* 27, no. 15 (August 1997): 1335–1358.

9. The *Wall Street Journal* reported that companies are following a trend of conducting culture audits as part of due diligence in determining merger compatibility. See "A Special Background Report on Trends in Industry and Finance," *Wall Street Journal*, 5 March 1998, p. 1.

10. See Cartwright and Cooper, "The Role of Culture Compatibility in Successful Organizational Marriage."

11. See S. Sleek, "Some Corporate Mergers, Like Marriages, End Up on the Rocks." Sleek points out that organizational psychologists try to help companies develop realistic expectations about a merger, just as they would help romantic partners anticipate some of the struggles they'll encounter after they marry.

CHAPTER 11

1. See J. J. Morrow and M. Stern, "Stars, Adversaries, Producers, and Phantoms at Work: A New Leadership Typology," in *Measures of Leadership*, ed. K. C. Clark and M. M. Clark (Greensboro, NC: Center for Creative Leadership, 1990), pp. 419–439. Morrow and Stern describe the results of IBM's Management Assessment Program and use the term "Dimensions" to describe behaviors deemed important for effective management performance at IBM.

2. See T. Bouchard's research on twins reared apart and his finding that 61% of leadership was genetically determined. See T. Bouchard, "All About Twins," *Newsweek*, 23 November 1987, p. 19.

3. J. M. Kouzes and B. Z. Posner claim that leadership is a learnable set of practices that anyone can master. See J. M. Kouzes and B. Z. Posner, *The Leadership Challenge: How to Get Extraordinary Things Done in Organizations* (San Francisco: Jossey-Bass, 1987).

4. These dimensions have demonstrated their importance to effective leadership in a number of studies. In my own study of over 200 senior-level executives, these dimensions consistently showed up on the effective executives' profile charts. See S. D. Truskie, "The President/CEO Study," research report published by Management Science and Development, Inc., Pittsburgh, PA, 1990.

5. J. P. Kotter reports on the importance of company knowledge, industry knowledge, and reputation and track record in executive leadership throughout his book *The Leadership Factor* (New York: The Free Press, 1988). The difference in complexity levels between executives and managers is presented in "Military Executive Leadership" by T. O. Jacobs and E. Jacques, in *Measures of Leadership*. This chapter includes Jacques' work of over 35 years of observational experience on the leadership requirements of various levels of the organization.

6. In comparing my dimensions, "The President/CEO Study," with those of D. N. Jackson, R. A. Hagberg, and D. N. Jackson III ("Dimensions of Executive Performance," paper presented at the Eighth Annual Conference of the Society for Industrial and Organizational Psychology, Inc., San Francisco, CA, 2 May 1993), there was much similarity between the lists. I combined the lists and assigned each dimension to the cultural pattern to which it demonstrated relevance.

7. See McCall, Lombardo, and Morrison, *The Lessons of Experience*.

Bibliography

Anastasi, A. *Psychological Testing*. New York: Macmillian, 1988.

Anderson, C. "Value-Based Management." *Academy of Management Executive* 11 (November 1997): 25–41.

Baxley, D. J. "IBM I/T Transformation Consortium Best Practices Benchmark." A report by IBM, Inc., 1996.

Beckard, R. *Organization Development: Strategies and Models*. Reading, MA: Addison-Wesley, 1969.

Beckard, R., and R. T. Harris. *Organizational Transitions: Managing Complex Change*. Reading, MA: Addison-Wesley, 1987.

Beckard, R., and W. Pritchard. *Changing the Essence: The Art of Creating Fundamental Change in Organizations*. San Francisco: Jossey-Bass, 1992.

Bianco, A., and S. Anderson. "Is Columbia/HCA's CEO on the Hit List?" *BusinessWeek*, 4 August 1997, in *BusinessWeek* Archives, pp. 1–5.

Bouchard, T. "All about Twins." *Newsweek*, 23 November 1987, p. 19.

Brannigan, M. "Delta Air's Allen to Quit Three Posts." *Wall Street Journal*, 13 May 1997, pp. A3–A4.

Brannigan, M., and J. S. Lublin. "Delta Airlines Changes Style with New Chief." *Wall Street Journal*, 18 August 1997, pp. B1–B2.

Burns, J. M. *Leadership*. New York: Harper & Row, 1978.

Calori, R., and P. Sarnin. "Corporate Culture and Economic Performance." *Organization Studies* 12 (1991): 49–74.

Cartwright, S., and C. L. Cooper. "The Role of Compatibility in Successful Organizational Marriage." *Academy of Management Executive* 7, no. 2 (1993): 57–69.

Chatman, J., and K. A. Jehn. "Assessing the Relationship between Industry Characteristics and Organizational Culture: How Different Can You Be?" *Academy of Management Journal* 37, no. 3 (June 1994): 522–553.

Choi, T. Y., and O. C. Behling. "Top Managers and TQM Success: One More

Look After All These Years." *Academy of Management Executive* 11 (1997): 37–47.

Church, A. H. "From Both Sides Now: Leadership—So Close and Yet So Far." *The Industrial Organizational Psychologist* 35 (January 1998): 57–69.

Clark, E. C., and M. M. Clark, eds. *Measures of Leadership*. Greensboro, NC: Center for Creative Leadership, 1990.

Collins, J. C., and J. I. Porras. "Building Your Company's Vision." *Harvard Business Review* (September/October 1996): 65–77.

Compaq Access. "Compaq's History." Accessed 1 April 1997. Available from http://www.compaq.com.

Davis, J. H., F. D. Schoorman, and L. Donaldson. "Toward a Stewardship Theory of Management." *Academy of Management Review* 22 (1997): 20–47.

Denison, D. "What Is the Difference between Organizational Culture and Organizational Climate? A Native's Point of View on a Decade of Paradigm Wars." *Academy of Management Review* 21 (1996): 619–654.

Duff, C., and B. Ortega. "How Wal-Mart Outdid a Once-Touted K-Mart in Discount Store Race." *Wall Street Journal*, 24 March 1995, pp. A1, A4.

Fitzgerald, C. "Type Development and Leadership Development." In *Developing Leaders*, ed. C. Fitzgerald and L. K. Kirby. New York: Davies-Black, 1997, pp. 311–335.

Flint, J. "Company of the Year." *Forbes*, 13 January 1997, cover story.

Freedman, A. M. "The Undiscussable Sides of Implementing Transformational Change." *Consulting Psychology Journal: Practice and Research* 49, no. 1 (Winter 1997): 51–76.

Frost, P. "Rekindling the Flame." Symposium presented at the annual meeting of the Academy of Management, San Diego, CA, 1985.

Gordon, G., and N. Ditomaso. "Predicting Corporate Performance from Organizational Culture." *Journal of Management Studies* 29 (1992): 783–798.

Hammer, M., and S. A. Stanton. "The Power of Reflection." *Fortune*, 24 November 1997, pp. 291–296.

Hansen, G., and B. Wernerfelt. "Determinants of Firm Performance: The Relative Importance of Economic and Organizational Factors." *Strategic Management Journal* 10 (1989): 399–411.

Herion, G., and T. Rossi. *Hartwick Leadership Cases: Jesus and the Gospels*. Oneonta, NY: The Hartwick Management Institute, 1993.

Hewlett-Packard Access. "The HP Way." Accessed 2 June 1998. Available from http://www.hp.com/abouthp/hpway.htm.

Intel Access. "Intel Mission and Values." Accessed 5 May 1998. Available from http://www.intel.com.

Jackson, D. N., R. A. Hagberg, and D. N. Jackson III. "Dimensions of Executive Performance." Paper presented at the Eighth Annual Conference of the Society for Industrial and Organizational Psychology, Inc., San Francisco, CA, 2 May 1993.

Jacobs, T. O., and E. Jacques. "Military Executive Leadership." In *Measures of Leadership*, ed. K. C. Clark and M. M. Clark. Greensboro, NC: Center for Creative Leadership, 1990.

Jaffe, G., and A. Sharpe. "Inside Booming Columbia Home-Care Business." *Wall Street Journal*, 9 October 1997, pp. B1–B2.

Judge, P. C. "Is It Rainforest Crunch Time at Ben & Jerry's?" *BusinessWeek*, 15 July 1996, in *BusinessWeek* Archives, pp. 1–2.

Kaplan, R. S., and D. P. Norton. "Using the Balanced Scoreboard as a Strategic Management System." *Harvard Business Review* (January/February 1996): 1–13.

King, W. R. "Westinghouse: What Went Wrong." *Pittsburgh Post-Gazette*, 15 March 1998, pp. C1, C4.

Kinlaw, D. C. *Developing Superior Work Teams*. Lexington, MA: Lexington Books, 1991.

Kirby, L. K. "Introduction: Psychological Type and the Myers-Briggs Type Indicator." In *Developing Leaders*, ed. C. Fitzgerald and L. K. Kirby. Palo Alto, CA: Davies-Black, 1997, pp. 3–31.

Kirkpatrick, D. "Intel's Amazing Profit Machine." *Fortune* [online]. Accessed 3 September 1998. Available from http://www.pathfinder.com/fortune/1997/970212/ tel.html.

Koestenbaum, P. *Leadership: The Inner Side of Greatness*. San Francisco: Jossey-Bass, 1991.

Kotter, J. P. *A Force for Change*. New York: The Free Press, 1990.

Kotter, J. P. *The Leadership Factor*. New York: The Free Press, 1988.

Kotter, J. P. *Leading Change*. Boston: Harvard Business School Press, 1996.

Kotter, J. P., and J. L. Heskett. *Corporate Culture and Performance*. New York: The Free Press, 1992.

Kouzes, J. M., and B. Z. Posner. *The Leadership Challenge: How to Get Extraordinary Things Done in Organizations*. San Francisco: Jossey-Bass, 1987.

Lagnado, L., E. M. Rodriquez, and G. Jaffe. "How 'Out of the Loop' Was Dr. Frist during Columbia's Expansion?" *Wall Street Journal*, 4 September 1997, pp. A1, A6.

Manz, C. C. "Self-Leadership: Toward an Expanded Theory of Self-Influence Processes in Organizations." *Academy of Management Review* 11 (1997): 20–47.

Marks, M. L., and P. H. Mirvis. *Joining Forces: Making One Plus One Equal Three in Mergers, Acquisitions, and Alliances*. San Francisco: Jossey-Bass, 1998.

Massey, S. "Who Killed Westinghouse?" *Pittsburgh Post-Gazette*, series appearing 28 February–7 March 1998.

McCall, M. W., Jr., M. M. Lombardo, and A. M. Morrison. *The Lessons of Experience*. Lexington, MA: Lexington Books, 1988.

Merck Access. "Merck & Co., Inc. Mission Statement." Accessed 7 July 1998. Available from http://www.merck.com.

Morrow, J. J., and M. Stern. "Stars, Adversaries, Producers, and Phantoms at Work: A New Leadership Typology." In *Measures of Leadership*, ed. K. C. Clark and M. M. Clark. Greensboro, NC: Center for Creative Leadership, 1990, pp. 419–439.

Mottola, G., S. Gaertner, and J. Dovidio. "How Groups Merge: The Effects of Merger Integration Patterns on Anticipated Commitment to the Merged Organization." *Journal of Applied Social Psychology* 27, no. 15 (August 1997): 1335–1358.

Myers, I. B. *Introduction to Type*, 5th ed. Palo Alto, CA: Consulting Psychologists Press, 1993.

Nevis, E. C. *Organizational Consulting: A Gestalt Approach.* Cleveland: Gestalt Institute of Cleveland Press, 1987.

Pereira, J. "Ben & Jerry's Finds New CEO in Gun Industry." *Wall Street Journal,* 3 January 1997, p. B1.

Pereira, J. "Ben & Jerry's to Post Earnings Rise of 39%, First Increase in Five Quarters." *Wall Street Journal,* 20 October 1997, p. B10.

Perls, F. S., R. F. Helferline, and P. Goodman. *Gestalt Therapy.* New York: Dell, 1951.

"Person or Organization as a Whole." *Gestalt Institute of Cleveland, 1998–1999 Catalog,* p. 1.

Petrock, F. "Corporate Culture Enhances Profiles." *HR Magazine* (November 1990): 64–65.

Pettigrew, A. "On Studying Organizational Culture." *Administrative Science Quarterly* 24 (1979): 570–581.

Prochaska, J. O., C. C. DiClemente, and J. C. Norcross. "In Search of How People Change: Applications to Addictive Behaviors." *American Psychologist* 27, no. 9 (September 1992): 1102–1114.

Quinn, R. E. *Beyond Rational Management.* San Francisco: Jossey-Bass, 1988.

Reger, R. K., J. V. Mullane, L. T. Gustafson, and S. M. DeMarie. "Creating Earthquakes to Change Organizational Mindsets." *Academy of Management Executive* 8 (November 1994): 31–41.

Robey, D. *Designing Organizations.* Homewood, IL: Irwin, 1991.

Rosenthal, T. L., and B. D. Steffek. "Modeling Methods." In *Helping People Change,* 4th ed., ed. F. H. Kanter and A. P. Goldstein. Boston: Allyn & Bacon, 1991, pp. 70–121.

Sager, I. "How IBM Became a Growth Company Again." *BusinessWeek,* 9 December 1996, cover story.

Sager, I., G. McWilliams, and A. Reinhardt. "IBM: Back to Double Digit Growth?" *BusinessWeek,* 1 June 1998, pp. 116–121.

Sashkin, M., and W. W. Burke. "Understanding and Assessing Organizational Leadership." In *Measures of Leadership,* ed. K. C. Clark and M. M. Clark. Greensboro, NC: Center for Creative Leadership, 1990, pp. 297–327.

Schein, E. *Organizational Culture and Leadership,* 2d ed. San Francisco: Jossey-Bass, 1992.

Schlender, B. "The New Man Inside Intel." *Fortune* [online]. Accessed 3 September 1998. Available from http://www.pathfinder.com/fortune/digitalwatch/0511fil.html.

Schneider, R., and R. A. Levine. *Culture Theory: Essays on Mind, Self, and Emotion.* Cambridge: Cambridge University Press, 1984.

Schroeder, M. "Why Steel Is Still Bent Out of Shape." *BusinessWeek,* 1 July 1991, in *BusinessWeek* Archives, pp. 1–3.

Scott, W. A. *Institutions and Organizations.* Thousand Oaks, CA: Sage Publications, 1995.

"Shareholder Scoreboard." *Wall Street Journal,* 26 February 1998, special section, pp. R1–R20.

Simons, R. "Control in an Age of Empowerment." *Harvard Business Review* (March/April 1995): 25–34.

Sleek, S. "Some Corporate Mergers, Like Marriages, End Up on the Rocks." *Monitor*, The American Psychological Association (July 1998): 13.

Slywotzky, A. J., and D. J. Morrison. *The Profit Zone: How Strategic Business Design Will Lead You to Tommorow's Profits*, New York: Random House, 1997.

Smith, G. "Life Won't Be Just a Bowl of Cherry Garcia." *BusinessWeek*, 18 July 1994, in *BusinessWeek* Archives, pp. 1–2.

Smith, H. In *The Illustrated World's Religions*. San Francisco: Harper, 1994.

"A Special Background Report on Trends in Industry and Finance." *Wall Street Journal*, 5 March 1998, p. 1.

Spencer, L. M., and S. M. Spencer. *Competence at Work*. New York: John Wiley & Sons, 1993.

Stewart, T. A. "America's Most Admired Companies." *Fortune*, 2 March 1998, pp. 70–82.

Stross, R. E., and W. Woods. "What's a High-Class Company Like Hewlett-Packard Doing in a Lowbrow Business Like PC's?" *Fortune* [online]. Accessed 5 May 1998. Available from http://www.pathfinder.com/fortune/1997/970929/hew.html.

Triandis, H. D. "The Psychological Measurement of Culture Syndromes." *American Psychologist* 51, no. 4 (1996): 407–415.

Truskie, S. D. "The Driving Force of Successful Organizations." *Business Horizons* (May/June 1984): 43–48.

Truskie, S. D. "The President/CEO Study." Research report published by Management Science and Development, Inc., Pittsburgh, PA, 1990.

Walck, C. L. "Using the MBTI in Management and Leadership." In *Developing Leaders*, ed. C. Fitzgerald and L. K. Kirby. Palo Alto, CA: Davies-Black, 1997, pp. 63–114.

Walton, S., with J. Huey. *Sam Walton: Made in America*. New York: Bantam Books, 1992.

Wheelwright, G. "The Near Fall and Rise of Compaq Computer." *TCP OnLine* 6, no. 1 (January 1997) [journal online]. Accessed 1 May 1998. Available from editorial@TCP.mindlink.bc.ca.

"World-Class Operations: Taking Care of What Takes Care of You." *Quality Management*, Bureau of Business Practice Newsletter, 25 June 1997, pp. 1–4.

Zaleznik, A. "Managers and Leaders: Are They Different?" *Harvard Business Review* 55, no. 5 (November/December 1977): 67–78.

Zatz, D. A. "Harnessing the Power of Change." *Ansom* (February 1994). Available from http://ssn.ssnlink.net/2zatzlodla/culture2.html.

Index

About the Author

STANLEY D. TRUSKIE is President and CEO of Management Science and Development, Inc., Pittsburgh, Pennsylvania, a consulting firm specializing in organizational effectiveness and leadership development. He recently served on the Blue Ribbon Commission on CEO Succession sponsored by the National Association of Corporate Directors. Dr. Truskie is a frequent speaker before organizations worldwide and a recognized researcher and author.